Life and Death

William Walker

ISBN: 978-0-244-36033-7

FOR THE WORLD

I

The offices of the Bureau of Population Equalization, vulgarly known as Popeek, were located on the twentieth through twenty-ninth floors of the Cullen Building, a hundred-story monstrosity typical of twenty-second-century neo-Victorian at its overdecorated worst. Roy Walton, Popeek's assistant administrator, had to apologize to himself each morning as he entered the hideous place.

Since taking the job, he had managed to redecorate his own office—on the twenty-eighth floor, immediately below Director FitzMaugham's—but that had created only one minor oasis in the esthetically repugnant building. It couldn't be helped, though; Popeek was unpopular, though necessary; and, like the public hangman of some centuries earlier, the Bureau did not rate attractive quarters.

So Walton had removed some of the iridescent chrome scalloping that trimmed the walls, replaced the sash windows with opaquers, and changed the massive ceiling fixture to more subtle electroluminescents. But the mark of the last century was stamped irrevocably on both building and office.

Which was as it should be, Walton had finally realized. It was the last century's foolishness that had made Popeek necessary, after all.

His desk was piled high with reports, and more kept arriving via pneumochute every minute. The job of assistant administrator was a thankless one, he thought; as much responsibility as Director FitzMaugham, and half the pay.

He lifted a report from one eyebrow-high stack, smoothed the crinkly paper carefully, and read it.

1

It was a despatch from Horrocks, the Popeek agent currently on duty in Patagonia. It was dated *4 June 2232*, six days before, and after a long and rambling prologue in the usual Horrocks manner it went on to say, *Population density remains low here: 17.3 per square mile, far below optimum. Looks like a prime candidate for equalization.*

Walton agreed. He reached for his voicewrite and said sharply, "Memo from Assistant Administrator Walton, re equalization of ..." He paused, picking a trouble-spot at random, "... central Belgium. Will the section chief in charge of this area please consider the advisability of transferring population excess to fertile areas in Patagonia? Recommendation: establishment of industries in latter region, to ease transition."

He shut his eyes, dug his thumbs into them until bright flares of light shot across his eyeballs, and refused to let himself be bothered by the multiple problems involved in dumping several hundred thousand Belgians into Patagonia. He forced himself to cling to one of Director FitzMaugham's oft-repeated maxims, *If you want to stay sane, think of these people as pawns in a chess game—not as human beings.*

Walton sighed. This was the biggest chess problem in the history of humanity, and the way it looked now, all the solutions led to checkmate in a century or less. They could keep equalizing population only so long, shifting like loggers riding logs in a rushing river, before trouble came.

There was another matter to be attended to now. He picked up the voicewrite again. "Memo from the assistant administrator, re establishment of new policy on reports from local agents: hire a staff of three clever girls to make a précis of each report, eliminating irrelevant data."

It was a basic step, one that should have been taken long ago. Now, with three feet of reports stacked on his desk, it was mandatory. One of the troubles with Popeek was its newness; it had been established so suddenly that most of its procedures were still in the formative stage.

He took another report from the heap. This one was the data sheet of the Zurich Euthanasia Center, and he gave it a cursory scanning. During the past week, eleven substandard children and twenty-three substandard adults had been sent on to Happysleep.

That was the grimmest form of population equalization. Walton initialed the report, earmarked it for files, and dumped it in the pneumochute.

The annunciator chimed.

"I'm busy," Walton said immediately.

"There's a Mr. Prior to see you," the annunciator's calm voice said. "He insists it's an emergency."

"Tell Mr. Prior I can't see anyone for at least three hours." Walton stared gloomily at the growing pile of paper on his desk. "Tell him he can have ten minutes with me at—oh, say, 1300."

Walton heard an angry male voice muttering something in the outer office, and then the annunciator said, "He insists he must see you immediately in reference to a Happysleep commitment."

"Commitments are irrevocable," Walton said heavily. The last thing in the world he wanted was to see a man whose child or parent had just been committed. "Tell Mr. Prior I can't see him at all."

Walton found his fingers trembling; he clamped them tight to the edge of his desk to steady himself. It was all right sitting up here in this ugly building and initialing commitment papers, but actually to *see* one of those people and try to convince him of the need—

The door burst open.

A tall, dark-haired man in an open jacket came rushing through and paused dramatically just over the threshold. Immediately behind him came three unsmiling men in the gray silk-sheen uniforms of security. They carried drawn needlers.

"Are you Administrator Walton?" the big man asked, in an astonishingly deep, rich voice. "I have to see you. I'm Lyle Prior."

The three security men caught up and swarmed all over Prior. One of them turned apologetically to Walton. "We're terribly sorry about this, sir. He just broke away and ran. We can't understand how he got in here, but he did."

"Ah—yes. So I noticed," Walton remarked drily. "See if he's planning to assassinate anybody, will you?"

"Administrator Walton!" Prior protested. "I'm a man of peace! How can you accuse me of—"

One of the security men hit him. Walton stiffened and resisted the urge to reprimand the man. He was only doing his job, after all.

"Search him," Walton said.

They gave Prior an efficient going-over. "He's clean, Mr. Walton. Should we take him to security, or downstairs to health?"

"Neither. Leave him here with me."

"Are you sure you—"

"Get out of here," Walton snapped. As the three security men slinked away, he added, "And figure out some more efficient system for protecting me. Some day an assassin is going to sneak through here and get me. Not that I give a damn about myself, you understand; it's simply that I'm indispensable. There isn't another lunatic in the world who'd take this job. Now *get out!*"

They wasted no time in leaving. Walton waited until the door closed and jammed down hard on the lockstud. His tirade, he knew, was wholly unjustified; if he had remembered to lock his door as regulations prescribed, Prior would never have broken in. But he couldn't admit that to the guards.

"Take a seat, Mr. Prior."

"I have to thank you for granting me this audience," Prior said, without a hint of sarcasm in his booming voice. "I realize you're a terribly busy man."

"I am." Another three inches of paper had deposited itself on Walton's desk since Prior had entered. "You're very lucky to have hit the psychological moment for your entrance. At any other time I'd have had you brigged for a month, but just now I'm in need of a little diversion. Besides, I very much admire your work, Mr. Prior."

"Thank you." Again that humility, startling in so big and commanding a man. "I hadn't expected to find—I mean that you—"

"That a bureaucrat should admire poetry? Is that what you're groping for?"

Prior reddened. "Yes," he admitted.

Grinning, Walton said, "I have to do *something* when I go home at night. I don't really read Popeek reports twenty-four hours a day. No more than twenty; that's my rule. I thought your last book was quite remarkable."

"The critics didn't," Prior said diffidently.

"Critics! What do they know?" Walton demanded. "They swing in cycles. Ten years ago it was form and technique, and you got the Melling Prize. Now it's message, political content that counts. That's not poetry, Mr. Prior—and there are still a few of us who recognize what poetry is. Take Yeats, for instance—"

Walton was ready to launch into a discussion of every poet from Prior back to Surrey and Wyatt; anything to keep from the job at hand, anything to keep his mind from Popeek. But Prior interrupted him.

"Mr. Walton...."

"Yes?"

"My son Philip ... he's two weeks old now...."

Walton understood. "No, Prior. Please don't ask." Walton's skin felt cold; his hands, tightly clenched, were clammy.

"He was committed to Happysleep this morning—potentially tubercular. The boy's perfectly sound, Mr. Walton. Couldn't you—"

Walton rose. "*No*," he said, half-commanding, half-pleading. "Don't ask me to do it. I can't make any exceptions, not even for you. You're an intelligent man; you understand our program."

"I voted for Popeek. I know all about Weeding the Garden and the Euthanasia Plan. But I hadn't expected—"

"You thought euthanasia was a fine thing for *other* people. So did everyone else," Walton said. "That's how the act was passed." Tenderly he said, "I can't do it. I can't spare your son. Our doctors give a baby every chance to live."

"*I* was tubercular. They cured me. What if they had practiced euthanasia a generation ago? Where would my poems be now?"

It was an unanswerable question; Walton tried to ignore it. "Tuberculosis is an extremely rare disease, Mr. Prior. We can wipe it out completely if we strike at those with TB-susceptible genetic traits."

"Meaning you'll kill any children I have?" Prior asked.

"Those who inherit your condition," Walton said gently. "Go home, Mr. Prior. Burn me in effigy. Write a poem about me. But don't ask me to do the impossible. I can't catch any falling stars for you."

Prior rose. He was immense, a hulking tragic figure staring broodingly at Walton. For the first time since the poet's abrupt entry, Walton feared violence. His fingers groped for the needle gun he kept in his upper left desk drawer.

But Prior had no violence in him. "I'll leave you," he said somberly. "I'm sorry, sir. Deeply sorry. For both of us."

Walton pressed the doorlock to let him out, then locked it again and slipped heavily into his chair. Three more reports slid out of the chute and landed on his desk. He stared at them as if they were three basilisks.

In the six weeks of Popeek's existence, three thousand babies had been ticketed for Happysleep, and three thousand sets of degenerate genes had been wiped from the race. Ten thousand subnormal males had been sterilized. Eight thousand dying oldsters had reached their graves ahead of time.

It was a tough-minded program. But why transmit palsy to unborn generations? Why let an adult idiot litter the world with subnormal progeny? Why force a man hopelessly cancerous to linger on in pain, consuming precious food?

Unpleasant? Sure. But the world had voted for it. Until Lang and his team succeeded in terraforming Venus, or until the faster-than-light outfit opened the stars to mankind, something had to be done about Earth's overpopulation. There were seven billion now and the figure was still growing.

Prior's words haunted him. *I was tubercular ... where would my poems be now?*

The big humble man was one of the great poets. Keats had been tubercular too.

What good are poets? he asked himself savagely.

The reply came swiftly: *What good is anything, then?* Keats, Shakespeare, Eliot, Yeats, Donne, Pound, Matthews ... and Prior. How much duller life would be without them, Walton thought, picturing his bookshelf—his one bookshelf, in his crowded little cubicle of a one-room home.

Sweat poured down his back as he groped toward his decision.

The step he was considering would disqualify him from his job if he admitted it, though he wouldn't do that. Under the Equalization Law, it would be a criminal act.

But just one baby wouldn't matter. Just one.

Prior's baby.

With nervous fingers he switched on the annunciator and said, "If there are any calls for me, take the message. I'll be out of my office for the next half-hour."

II

He stepped out of the office, glancing around furtively. The outer office was busy: half a dozen girls were answering calls, opening letters, coordinating activities. Walton slipped quickly past them into the hallway.

There was a knot of fear in his stomach as he turned toward the lift tube. Six weeks of pressure, six weeks of tension since Popeek was organized and old man FitzMaugham had tapped him for the second-in-command post ... and now, a rebellion. The sparing of a single child was a small rebellion, true, but he knew he was striking as effectively at the base of Popeek this way as if he had brought about repeal of the entire Equalization Law.

Well, just one lapse, he promised himself. I'll spare Prior's child, and after that I'll keep within the law.

He jabbed the lift tube indicator and the tube rose in its shaft. The clinic was on the twentieth floor.

"Roy."

At the sound of the quiet voice behind him, Walton jumped in surprise. He steadied himself, forcing himself to turn slowly. The director stood there.

"Good morning, Mr. FitzMaugham."

The old man was smiling serenely, his unlined face warm and friendly, his mop of white hair bright and full. "You look preoccupied, boy. Something the matter?"

Walton shook his head quickly. "Just a little tired, sir. There's been a lot of work lately."

As he said it, he knew how foolish it sounded. If anyone in Popeek worked harder than he did, it was the elderly director. FitzMaugham had striven for equalization legislation for fifty years, and now, at the age of eighty, he put in a sixteen-hour day at the task of saving mankind from itself.

The director smiled. "You never did learn how to budget your strength, Roy. You'll be a worn-out wreck before you're half my age. I'm glad you're adopting my habit of taking a coffee break in the morning, though. Mind if I join you?"

"I'm—not taking a break, sir. I have some work to do downstairs."

"Oh? Can't you take care of it by phone?"

"No, Mr. FitzMaugham." Walton felt as though he'd already been tried, drawn, and quartered. "It requires personal attention."

"I see." The deep, warm eyes bored into his. "You ought to slow down a little, I think."

"Yes, sir. As soon as the work eases up a little."

FitzMaugham chuckled. "In another century or two, you mean. I'm afraid you'll never learn how to relax, my boy."

The lift tube arrived. Walton stepped to one side, allowed the Director to enter, and got in himself. FitzMaugham pushed *Fourteen*; there was a coffee shop down there. Hesitantly, Walton pushed *twenty*, covering the panel with his arm so the old man would be unable to see his destination.

As the tube began to descend, FitzMaugham said, "Did Mr. Prior come to see you this morning?"

"Yes," Walton said.

"He's the poet, isn't he? The one you say is so good?"

"That's right, sir," Walton said tightly.

"He came to see me first, but I had him referred down to you. What was on his mind?"

Walton hesitated. "He—he wanted his son spared from Happysleep. Naturally, I had to turn him down."

"Naturally," FitzMaugham agreed solemnly. "Once we make even one exception, the whole framework crumbles."

"Of course, sir."

The lift tube halted and rocked on its suspension. The door slid back, revealing a neat, gleaming sign:

FLOOR 20
Euthanasia Clinic and Files

Walton had forgotten the accursed sign. He began to wish he had avoided traveling down with the director. He felt that his purpose must seem nakedly obvious now.

The old man's eyes were twinkling amusedly. "I guess you get off here," he said. "I hope you catch up with your work soon, Roy. You really should take some time off for relaxation each day."

"I'll try, sir."

Walton stepped out of the tube and returned FitzMaugham's smile as the door closed again. Bitter thoughts assailed him as soon as he was alone.

Some fine criminal you are. You've given the show away already! And damn that smooth paternal smile. FitzMaugham knows! He must know!

Walton wavered, then abruptly made his decision. He sucked in a deep breath and walked briskly toward the big room where the euthanasia files were kept.

The room was large, as rooms went nowadays—thirty by twenty, with deck upon deck of Donnerson micro-memory-tubes racked along one wall and a bank of microfilm records along the other. In six weeks of life Popeek had piled up an impressive collection of data.

While he stood there, the computer chattered, lights flashed. New facts poured into the memory banks. It probably went on day and night.

"Can I help—oh, it's you, Mr. Walton," a white-smocked technician said. Popeek employed a small army of technicians, each one faceless and without personality, but always ready to serve. "Is there anything I can do?"

"I'm simply running a routine checkup. Mind if I use the machine?"

"Not at all, sir. Go right ahead."

Walton grinned lightly and stepped forward. The technician practically backed out of his presence.

No doubt I must radiate charisma, he thought. Within the building he wore a sort of luminous halo, by virtue of being Director FitzMaugham's protégé and second-in-command. Outside, in the colder reality of the crowded metropolis, he kept his identity and Popeek rank quietly to himself.

Frowning, he tried to remember the Prior boy's name. Ah ... Philip, wasn't it? He punched out a request for the card on Philip Prior.

A moment's pause followed, while the millions of tiny cryotronic circuits raced with information pulses, searching the Donnerson tubes for Philip Prior's record. Then, a brief squeaking sound and a yellow-brown card dropped out of the slot:

3216847AB1

PRIOR, *Philip Hugh. Born 31 May 2232, New York General Hospital, New York. First son of Prior, Lyle Martin and Prior, Ava Leonard. Wgt. at birth 5lb. 3oz.*

An elaborate description of the boy in great detail followed, ending with blood type, agglutinating characteristic, and gene-pattern, codified. Walton skipped impatiently through that and came to the notification typed in curt, impersonal green capital letters at the bottom of the card:

EXAMINED AT N Y EUTH CLINIC 10 JUNE 2332
EUTHANASIA RECOMMENDED

He glanced at his watch: the time was 1026. The boy was probably still somewhere in the clinic lab, waiting for the figurative axe to descend.

Walton had set up the schedule himself: the gas chamber delivered Happysleep each day at 1100 and 1500. He had about half an hour to save Philip Prior.

He peered covertly over his shoulder; no one was in sight. He slipped the baby's card into his breast pocket.

That done, he typed out a requisition for explanation of the gene-sorting code the clinic used. Symbols began pouring forth, and Walton puzzledly correlated them with the line of gibberish on Phillip Prior's record card. Finally he found the one he wanted: *3f2, tubercular-prone.*

He scrapped the guide sheet he had and typed out a message to the machine. *Revision of card number 3216847AB1 follows. Please alter in all circuits.*

He proceeded to retype the child's card, omitting both the fatal symbol *3f2*and the notation recommending euthanasia from the new version. The machine beeped an acknowledgement. Walton smiled. So far, so good.

Then, he requested the boy's file all over again. After the customary pause, a card numbered 3216847AB1 dropped out of the slot. He read it.

The deletions had been made. As far as the machine was concerned, Philip Prior was a normal, healthy baby.

He glanced at his watch. 1037. Still twenty-three minutes before this morning's haul of unfortunates was put away.

Now came the real test: could he pry the baby away from the doctors without attracting too much attention to himself in the process?

———————

Five doctors were bustling back and forth as Walton entered the main section of the clinic. There must have been a hundred babies there, each in a little pen of its own, and the doctors were humming from one to the next, while anxious parents watched from screens above.

The Equalization Law provided that every child be presented at its local clinic within two weeks of birth, for an examination and a certificate. Perhaps one in ten thousand would be denied a certificate ... and life.

"Hello, Mr. Walton. What brings you down here?"

Walton smiled affably. "Just a routine investigation, Doctor. I try to keep in touch with every department we have, you know."

"Mr. FitzMaugham was down here to look around a little while ago. We're really getting a going-over today, Mr. Walton!"

"Umm. Yes." Walton didn't like that, but there was nothing he could do about it. He'd have to rely on the old man's abiding faith in his protégé to pull him out of any possible stickiness that arose.

"Seen my brother around?" he asked.

"Fred? He's working in room seven, running analyses. Want me to get him for you, Mr. Walton?"

"No—no, don't bother him, thanks. I'll find him later." Inwardly, Walton felt relieved. Fred Walton, his younger brother, was a doctor in the employ of Popeek. Little love was lost between the brothers, and Roy did not care to have Fred know he was down there.

Strolling casually through the clinic, he peered at a few plump, squalling babies, and said, "Find many sour ones today?"

"Seven so far. They're scheduled for the 1100 chamber. Three tuberc, two blind, one congenital syph."

"That only makes six," Walton said.

"Oh, and a spastic," the doctor said. "Biggest haul we've had yet. Seven in one morning."

"Have any trouble with the parents?"

"What do you think?" the doctor asked. "But some of them seemed to understand. One of the tuberculars nearly raised the roof, though."

Walton shuddered. "You remember his name?" he asked, with feigned calm.

Silence for a moment. "No. Darned if I can think of it. I can look it up for you if you like."

"Don't bother," Walton said hurriedly.

He moved on, down the winding corridor that led to the execution chamber. Falbrough, the executioner, was studying a list of names at his desk when Walton appeared.

Falbrough didn't look like the sort of man who would enjoy his work. He was short and plump, with a high-domed bald head and glittering contact lenses in his weak blue eyes. "Morning, Mr. Walton."

"Good morning, Doctor Falbrough. You'll be operating soon, won't you?"

"Eleven hundred, as usual."

"Good. There's a new regulation in effect from now on," Walton said. "To keep public opinion on our side."

"Sir?"

"Henceforth, until further notice, you're to check each baby that comes to you against the main file, just to make sure there's been no mistake. Got that?"

"*Mistake?* But how—"

"Never mind that, Falbrough. There was quite a tragic slip-up at one of the European centers yesterday. We may all hang for it if news gets out." *How glibly I reel this stuff off,* Walton thought in amazement.

Falbrough looked grave. "I see, sir. Of course. We'll double-check everything from now on."

"Good. Begin with the 1100 batch."

Walton couldn't bear to remain down in the clinic any longer. He left via a side exit, and signaled for a lift tube.

Minutes later he was back in his office, behind the security of a towering stack of work. His pulse was racing; his throat was dry. He remembered what FitzMaugham had said: *Once we make even one exception, the whole framework crumbles.*

Well, the framework had begun crumbling, then. And there was little doubt in Walton's mind that FitzMaugham knew or would soon know what he had done. He would have to cover his traces, somehow.

The annunciator chimed and said, "Dr. Falbrough of Happysleep calling you, sir."

"Put him on."

The screen lit and Falbrough's face appeared; its normal blandness had given way to wild-eyed tenseness.

"What is it, Doctor?"

"It's a good thing you issued that order when you did, sir! You'll never guess what just happened—"

"No guessing games, Falbrough. Speak up."

"I—well, sir, I ran checks on the seven babies they sent me this morning. And guess—I mean—well, one of them shouldn't have been sent to me!"

"No!"

"It's the truth, sir. A cute little baby indeed. I've got his card right here. The boy's name is Philip Prior, and his gene-pattern is fine."

"Any recommendation for euthanasia on the card?" Walton asked.

"No, sir."

Walton chewed at a ragged cuticle for a moment, counterfeiting great anxiety. "Falbrough, we're going to have to keep this very quiet. Someone slipped up in the examining room, and if word gets out that there's been as much as one mistake, we'll have a mob swarming over us in half an hour."

"Yes, sir." Falbrough looked terribly grave. "What should I do, sir?"

"Don't say a word about this to *anyone*, not even the men in the examining room. Fill out a certificate for the boy, find his parents, apologize and return him to them. And make sure you keep checking for any future cases of this sort."

"Certainly, sir. Is that all?"

"It is," Walton said crisply, and broke the contact. He took a deep breath and stared bleakly at the far wall.

The Prior boy was safe. And in the eyes of the law—the Equalization Law—Roy Walton was now a criminal. He was every bit as much a criminal as the man who tried to hide his dying father from the investigators, or the anxious parents who attempted to bribe an examining doctor.

He felt curiously dirty. And, now that he had betrayed FitzMaugham and the Cause, now that it was done, he had little idea why he had done it, why he had jeopardized the Popeek program, his position—his life, even—for the sake of one potentially tubercular baby.

Well, the thing was done.

No. Not quite. Later, when things had quieted down, he would have to finish the job by transferring all the men in the clinic to distant places and by obliterating the computer's memories of this morning's activities.

The annunciator chimed again. "Your brother is on the wire, sir."

Walton trembled imperceptibly as he said, "Put him on." Somehow, Fred never called unless he could say or do something unpleasant. And Walton was very much afraid that his brother meant no good by this call. No good at all.

III

Roy Walton watched his brother's head and shoulders take form out of the swirl of colors on the screen. Fred Walton was more compact, built closer to the ground than his rangy brother; he was a squat five-seven, next to Roy's lean six-two. Fred had always threatened to "get even" with his older brother as soon as they were the same size, but to Fred's great dismay he had never managed to catch up with Roy in height.

Even on the screen, Fred's neck and shoulders gave an impression of tremendous solidity and force. Walton waited for his brother's image to take shape, and when the time lag was over he said, "Well, Fred? What goes?"

His brother's eyes flickered sleepily. "They tell me you were down here a little while ago, Roy. How come I didn't rate a visit?"

"I wasn't in your section. It was official business, anyway. I didn't have time."

Walton fixed his eyes sharply on the caduceus emblem gleaming on Fred's lapel, and refused to look anywhere else.

Fred said slowly, "You had time to tinker with our computer, though."

"Official business!"

"Really, Roy?" His brother's tone was venomous. "I happened to be using the computer shortly after you this morning. I was curious—unpardonably so, dear brother. I requested a transcript of your conversation with the machine."

Sparks seemed to flow from the screen. Walton sat back, feeling numb. He managed to pull his sagging mouth back into a stiff hard line and say, "That's a criminal offense, Fred. Any use I make of a Popeek computer outlet is confidential."

"Criminal offence? Maybe so ... but that makes two of us, then. Eh, Roy?"

"How much do you know?"

"You wouldn't want me to recite it over a public communications system, would you? Your friend FitzMaugham might be listening to every word of this, and I have too much fraternal feeling for that. Ole Doc Walton doesn't want to get his bigwig big brother in trouble—oh, no!"

"Thanks for small blessings," Roy said acidly.

"You got me this job. You can take it away. Let's call it even for now, shall we?"

"Anything you like," Walton said. He was drenched in sweat, though the ingenious executive filter in the sending apparatus of the screen cloaked that fact and presented him as neat and fresh. "I have some work to do now." His voice was barely audible.

"I won't keep you any longer, then," Fred said.

The screen went dead.

Walton killed the contact at his end, got up, walked to the window. He nudged the opaquer control and the frosty white haze over the glass cleared away, revealing the fantastic beehive of the city outside.

Idiot! he thought. *Fool!*

He had risked everything to save one baby, one child probably doomed to an early death anyway. And FitzMaugham knew—the old man could see through Walton with ease—and Fred knew, too. His brother, and his father-substitute.

FitzMaugham might well choose to conceal Roy's defection this time, but would surely place less trust in him in the future. And as for Fred....

There was no telling what Fred might do. They had never been particularly close as brothers; they had lived with their parents (now almost totally forgotten) until Roy was nine and Fred seven. Their parents had gone down off Maracaibo in a jet crash; Roy and Fred had been sent to the public crèche.

After that it had been separate paths for the brothers. For Roy, an education in the law, a short spell as Senator FitzMaugham's private secretary, followed last month by his sudden elevation to assistant administrator of the newly-created Popeek Bureau. For Fred, medicine, unsuccessful private practice, finally a job in the Happysleep section of Popeek, thanks to Roy.

And now he has the upper hand for the first time, Walton thought. *I hope he's not thirsting for my scalp.*

He was being ground in a vise; he saw now the gulf between the toughness needed for a Popeek man and the very real streak of softness that was part of his character. Walton suddenly realized that he had never merited his office. His only honorable move would be to offer his resignation to FitzMaugham at once.

He thought back, thought of the Senator saying, *This is a job for a man with no heart. Popeek is the cruelest organization ever legislated by man. You think you can handle it, Roy?*

I think so, sir. I hope so.

He remembered going on to declare some fuzzy phrases about the need for equalization, the immediate necessity for dealing with

Earth's population problem.

Temporary cruelty is the price of eternal happiness, FitzMaugham had said.

Walton remembered the day when the United Nations had finally agreed, had turned the Population Equalization Bureau loose on a stunned world. There had been the sharp flare of flash guns, the clatter of reporters feeding the story to the world, the momentary high-mindedness, the sense of the nobility of Popeek....

And then the six weeks of gathering hatred. No one liked Popeek. No one liked to put antiseptic on wounds, either, but it had to be done.

Walton shook his head sorrowfully. He had made a serious mistake by saving Philip Prior. But resigning his post was no way to atone for it.

He opaqued the window again and returned to his desk. It was time to go through the mail.

The first letter on the stack was addressed to him by hand; he slit it open and scanned it.

Dear Mr Walton,

Yesterday your men came and took away my mother to be kild. She didn't do nothing and lived a good life for seventy years and I want you to know I think you people are the biggest vermin since Hitler and Stalin and when youre old and sick I hope your own men come for you and stick you in the furnace where you belong. You stink and all of you stink.

Signed, *Disgusted*

Walton shrugged and opened the next letter, typed in a crisp voicewrite script on crinkly watermarked paper.

Sir:

I see by the papers that the latest euthanasia figures are the highest yet, and that you have successfully rid the world of many of its weak sisters, those who are unable to stand the gaff, those who, in the words of the immortal Darwin "are not fit to survive." My heartiest congratulations, sir, upon the scope and ambition of your bold and courageous program. Your Bureau offers mankind its first real chance to enter that promised land, that Utopia, that has been our hope and prayer for so long.

I do sincerely hope, though, that your Bureau is devoting careful thought to the type of citizen that should be spared. It seems obvious that the myriad spawning Asiatics should be reduced tremendously, since their unchecked proliferation has caused such great hardship to humanity. The same might be said of the

Europeans who refuse to obey the demands of sanity; and, coming closer to home, I pray you reduce the numbers of Jews, Catholics, Communists, anti-Herschelites, and other freethinking rabble, in order to make the new reborn world purer and cleaner and ...

With a sickly cough Walton put the letter down. Most of them were just this sort: intelligent, rational, bigoted letters. There had been the educated Alabamian, disturbed that Popeek did not plan to eliminate all forms of second-class citizens; there had been the Michigan minister, anxious that no left-wing relativistic atheists escape the gas chamber.

And, of course, there were the other kind—the barely literate letters from bereaved parents or relatives, accusing Popeek of nameless crimes against humanity.

Well, it was only to be expected, Walton thought. He scribbled his initials on both the letters and dropped them into the chute that led to files, where they would be put on microfilm and scrupulously stored away. FitzMaugham insisted that every letter received be read and so filed.

Some day soon, Walton thought, population equalization would be unnecessary. Oh, sure, euthanasia would stick; it was a sane and, in the long run, merciful process. But this business of uprooting a few thousand Belgians and shipping them to the open spaces in Patagonia would cease.

Lang and his experimenters were struggling to transform Venus into a livable world. If it worked, the terraforming engineers could go on to convert Mars, the bigger moons of Jupiter and Saturn, and perhaps even distant Pluto, if some form of heating could be developed.

There would be another transition then. Earth's multitudes would be shipped wholesale to the new worlds. Perhaps there would be riots; none but a few adventurers would go willingly. But some would go, and that would be a partial solution.

And then, the stars. The faster-than-light project was top secret, so top secret that in Popeek only FitzMaugham knew what was being done on it. But if it came through....

Walton shrugged and turned back to his work. Reports had to be read, filed, expedited.

The thought of Fred and what Fred knew bothered him. If only there were some way to relive this morning, to let the Prior baby go to the chamber as it deserved....

Tension pounded in him. He slipped a hand into his desk, fumbled, found the green, diamond-shaped pellet he was searching for, and swallowed the benzolurethrin almost unthinkingly. The tranquilizer was only partly successful in relaxing him, but he was able to work steadily, without a break, until noon.

He was about to dial for lunch when the private screen he and FitzMaugham used between their offices glowed into life.

"Roy?"

The director's face looked impossibly tranquil.

"Sir?"

"I'm going to have a visitor at 1300. Ludwig. He wants to know how things are going."

Walton nodded. Ludwig was the head American delegate to the United Nations, a stubborn, dedicated man who had fought Popeek for years; then he had seen the light and had fought just as strenuously for its adoption. "Do you want me to prepare a report for him?" Walton asked.

"No, Roy. I want you to be here. I don't want to face him alone."

"Sir?"

"Some of the UN people feel I'm running Popeek as a one-man show," FitzMaugham explained. "Of course, that's not so, as that mountain of work on your desk testifies. But I want you there as evidence of the truth. I want him to see how much I have to rely on my assistants."

"I get it. Very good, Mr. FitzMaugham."

"And another thing," the Director went on. "It'll help appearances if I show myself surrounded with loyal young lieutenants of impeccable character. Like you, Roy."

"Thank you, sir," Walton said weakly.

"Thank *you*. See you at 1300 sharp, then?"

"Of course, sir."

The screen went dead. Walton stared at it blankly. He wondered if this were some elaborate charade of the old man's; FitzMaugham was devious enough. That last remark, about loyal young lieutenants of impeccable character ... it had seemed to be in good faith, but was it? Was FitzMaugham staging an intricate pretense before deposing his faithless protégé?

Maybe Fred had something to do with it, Walton thought. He

decided to have another session with the computer after his conference with FitzMaugham and Ludwig. Perhaps it still wasn't too late to erase the damning data and cover his mistake.

Then it would be just his word against Fred's. He might yet be able to brazen through, he thought dully.

He ordered lunch with quivering fingers, and munched drearily on the tasteless synthetics for awhile before dumping them down the disposal chute.

IV

At precisely 1255 Walton tidied his desk, rose and for the second time that day, left his office. He was apprehensive, but not unduly so; behind his immediate surface fears and tensions lay a calm certainty that FitzMaugham ultimately would stick by him.

And there was little to fear from Fred, he realized now. It was next to impossible for a mere lower-level medic to gain the ear of the director himself; in the normal course of events, if Fred attempted to contact FitzMaugham, he would automatically be referred to Roy.

No; the danger in Fred's knowledge was potential, not actual, and there might still be time to come to terms with him. It was almost with a jaunty step that Walton left his office, made his way through the busy outer office, and emerged in the outside corridor.

Fred was waiting there.

He was wearing his white medic's smock, stained yellow and red by reagents and coagulants. He was lounging against the curving plastine corridor wall, hands jammed deep into his pockets. His thick-featured, broad face wore an expression of elaborate casualness.

"Hello, Roy. Fancy finding *you* here!"

"How did you know I'd be coming this way?"

"I called your office. They told me you were on your way to the lift tubes. Why so jumpy, brother? Have a tough morning?"

"I've had worse," Walton said. He was tense, guarded. He pushed the stud beckoning the lift tube.

"Where you off to?" Fred asked.

"Confidential. Top-level powwow with Fitz, if you have to know."

Fred's eyes narrowed. "Strictly upper-echelon, aren't you? Do you have a minute to talk to a mere mortal?"

"Fred, don't make unnecessary trouble. You know—"

"*Can it.* I've only got a minute or two left of my lunch hour. I want to make myself perfectly plain with you. Are there any spy pickups in this corridor?"

Walton considered that. There were none that he knew of, and he knew of most. Still, FitzMaugham might have found it advisable to plant a few without advertising the fact. "I'm not sure," he said. "What's on your mind?"

Fred took a pad from his pocket and began to scrawl a note. Aloud he said, "I'll take my chances and tell you about it anyway. One of the men in the lab said another man told him you and FitzMaugham are both secretly Herschelites." His brow furrowed with the effort of saying one thing and writing another simultaneously. "Naturally, I won't give you any names yet, but I want you to know I'm investigating his background very carefully. He may just have been shooting his mouth off."

"Is that why you didn't want this to go into a spy pickup?" Walton asked.

"Exactly. I prefer to investigate unofficially for the time being." Fred finished the note, ripped the sheet from the pad and handed it to his brother.

Walton read it wordlessly. The handwriting was jagged and untidy, for it was no easy feat to carry on a conversation for the benefit of any concealed pickups while writing a message.

It said, *I know all about the Prior baby. I'll keep my mouth shut for now, so don't worry. But don't try anything foolish, because I've deposited an account of the whole thing where you can't find it.*

Walton crumpled the note and tucked it into his pocket. He said,

"Thanks for the information, Fred. I'll keep it in mind."

"Okay, pal."

The lift tube arrived. Walton stepped inside and pressed *twenty-nine*.

In the moment it took for the tube to rise the one floor, he thought, *So Fred's playing a waiting game.... He'll hold the information over my head until he can make good use of it.*

That was some relief, anyway. No matter what evidence Fred had already salted away, Walton still had a chance to blot out some of the computer's memory track and obscure the trail to that extent.

———

The lift tube opened; a gleaming sign listed the various activities of the twenty-ninth floor, and at the bottom of the list it said *D. F. FitzMaugham, Director.*

FitzMaugham's office was at the back of a maze of small cubicles housing Popeek functionaries of one sort or another. Walton had made some attempt to familiarize himself with the organizational stratification of Popeek, but his success thus far had been minimal. FitzMaugham had conceived the plan half a century ago, and had lovingly created and worked over the organization's structure through all the long years it took before the law was finally passed.

There were plenty of bugs in the system, but in general FitzMaugham's blueprint had been sound—sound enough for Popeek to begin functioning almost immediately after its UN approval. The manifold departments, the tight network of inter-reporting agencies, the fantastically detailed budget with its niggling appropriations for office supplies and its massive expenditures for, say, the terraforming project—most of these were fully understood only by FitzMaugham himself.

Walton glanced at his watch. He was three minutes late; the conversation with his brother had delayed him. But Ludwig of the UN was not known to be a scrupulously punctual man, and there was a high probability he hadn't arrived.

The secretary in the office guarding FitzMaugham's looked up as Walton approached. "The director is in urgent conference, sir, and— oh, I'm sorry, Mr. Walton. Go right in; Mr. FitzMaugham is expecting you."

"Is Mr. Ludwig here yet?"

"Yes, sir. He arrived about ten minutes ago."

Curious, Walton thought. From what he knew of Ludwig he wasn't the man to arrive early for an appointment. Walton and FitzMaugham had had plenty of dealings with him in the days before Popeek was approved, and never once had Ludwig been on time.

Walton shrugged. If Ludwig could switch his stand so decisively from an emphatic anti-Popeek to an even more emphatic pro-Popeek, perhaps he could change in other respects as well.

Walton stepped within the field of the screener. His image, he knew, was being relayed inside where FitzMaugham could scrutinize him carefully before admitting him. The director was very touchy about admitting people to his office.

Five seconds passed; it usually took no more than that for FitzMaugham to admit him. But there was no sign from within, and Walton coughed discreetly.

Still no answer. He turned away and walked over to the desk where the secretary sat dictating into a voicewrite. He waited for her to finish her sentence, then touched her arm lightly.

"Yes, Mr. Walton?"

"The screen transmission seems to be out of order. Would you mind calling Mr. FitzMaugham on the annunciator and telling him I'm here?"

"Of course, sir."

Her fingers deftly flipped the switches. He waited for her to announce him, but she paused and looked back at Walton. "He doesn't acknowledge, Mr. Walton. He must be awfully busy."

"He *has* to acknowledge. Ring him again."

"I'm sorry, sir, but—"

"*Ring him again.*"

She rang, reluctantly, without any response. FitzMaugham preferred the sort of annunciator that had to be acknowledged; Walton allowed the girl to break in on his privacy without the formality of a return buzz.

"Still no answer, sir."

Walton was growing impatient. "Okay, devil take the acknowledgment. Break in on him and tell him I'm waiting out here. My presence is important inside."

"Sir, Mr. FitzMaugham absolutely forbids anyone to use the annunciator without his acknowledgment," the girl protested.

He felt his neck going red. "I'll take the responsibility."

"I'm sorry, sir—"

"All right. Get away from that machine and let *me* talk to him. If there are repercussions, tell him I forced you at gunpoint."

She backed away, horrified, and he slid in behind the desk. He made contact; there was no acknowledgment. He said, "Mr. FitzMaugham, this is Roy. I'm outside your office now. Should I come in, or not?"

Silence. He stared thoughtfully at the apparatus.

"I'm going in there," he said.

The door was of solid-paneled imitation wood, a couple of inches thick and probably filled with a good sturdy sheet of beryllium steel. FitzMaugham liked protection.

Walton contemplated the door for a moment. Stepping into the screener field, he said, "Mr. FitzMaugham? Can you hear me?" In the ensuing silence he went on, "This is Walton. I'm outside with a blaster, and unless I get any orders to the contrary, I'm going to break into your office."

Silence. This was very extraordinary indeed. He wondered if it were part of some trap of FitzMaugham's. Well, he'd find out soon enough. He adjusted the blaster aperture to short-range wide-beam, and turned it on. A soft even flow of heat bathed the door.

Quite a crowd of curious onlookers had gathered by now, at a respectful distance. Walton maintained the steady heat. The synthetic wood was sloughing away in dribbly blue masses as the radiation broke it down; the sheet of metal in the heart of the door was gleaming bright red.

The lock became visible now. Walton concentrated the flame there, and the door creaked and groaned.

He snapped the blaster off, pocketed it, and kicked the door soundly. It swung open.

He had a momentary glimpse of a blood-soaked white head slumped over a broad desk—and then someone hit him amidships.

He was a man about his own height, wearing a blue suit woven through with glittering gold threads; Walton's mind caught the details with odd clarity. The man's face was distorted with fear and shock, but Walton recognized it clearly enough. The ruddy cheeks, the broad nose and bushy eyebrows, belonged to Ludwig.

The UN man. The man who had just assassinated Director FitzMaugham.

He was battering his fists into Walton, struggling to get past him and through the wrecked door, to escape somewhere, anywhere. Walton grunted as a fist crashed into his stomach. He reeled backward, gagging and gasping, but managed to keep his hand on the other's coat. Desperately he pulled Ludwig to him. In the suddenness of the encounter he had no time to evaluate what had happened, no time to react to FitzMaugham's murder.

His one thought was that Ludwig had to be subdued.

His fist cracked into the other's mouth; sharp pain shot up through his hand at the impact of knuckles against teeth. Ludwig sagged. Walton realized that he was blocking the doorway; not only was he preventing Ludwig from escaping, he was also making it impossible for anyone outside to come to his own aid.

Blindly he clubbed his fist down on Ludwig's neck, spun him around, crashed another blow into the man's midsection. Suddenly Ludwig pulled away from him and ran back behind the director's desk.

Walton followed him ... and stopped short as he saw the UN man pause, quiver tremulously, and topple to the floor. He sprawled grotesquely on the deep beige carpet, shook for a moment, then was still.

Walton gasped for breath. His clothes were torn, he was sticky with sweat and blood, his heart was pounding from unaccustomed exertion.

Ludwig's killed the director, he thought leadenly. *And now Ludwig's dead.*

He leaned against the doorpost. He was conscious of figures moving past him, going into the room, examining FitzMaugham and the figure on the floor.

"Are you all right?" a crisp, familiar voice asked.

"Pretty winded," Walton admitted.

"Have some water."

Walton accepted the drink, gulped it, looked up at the man who had spoken. "Ludwig! How in hell's name—"

"A double," the UN man said. "Come over here and look at him."

Ludwig led him to the pseudo-Ludwig on the floor. It was an

incredible resemblance. Two or three of the office workers had rolled the body over; the jaws were clenched stiffly, the face frozen in an agonized mask.

"He took poison," Ludwig said. "I don't imagine he expected to get out of here alive. But he did his work well. God, I wish I'd been on time for once in my life!"

Walton glanced numbly from the dead Ludwig on the floor to the live one standing opposite him. His shocked mind realized dimly what had happened. The assassin, masked to look like Ludwig, had arrived at 1300, and had been admitted to the director's office. He had killed the old man, and then had remained inside the office, either hoping to make an escape later in the day, or perhaps simply waiting for the poison to take effect.

"It was bound to happen," Ludwig said. "They've been gunning for the senator for years. And now that Popeek was passed...."

Walton looked involuntarily at the desk, mirror bright and uncluttered as always. Director FitzMaugham was sprawled forward, hands half-clenched, arms spread. His impressive mane of white hair was stained with his own blood. He had been clubbed—the simplest, crudest sort of murder.

Emotional reaction began. Walton wanted to break things, to cry, to let off steam somehow. But there were too many people present; the office, once sacrosanct, had miraculously become full of Popeek workers, policemen, secretaries, possibly some telefax reporters.

Walton recovered a shred of his authority. "All of you, *outside!*" he said loudly. He recognized Sellors, the building's security chief, and added, "Except you, Sellors. You can stay here."

The crowd melted away magically. Now there were just five in the office—Sellors, Ludwig, Walton, and the two corpses.

Ludwig said, "Do you have any idea who might be behind this, Mr. Walton?"

"I don't know," he said wearily. "There are thousands who'd have wanted to kill the director. Maybe it was a Herschelite plot. There'll be a full investigation."

"Mind stepping out of the way, sir?" Sellors asked. "I'd like to take some photos."

Walton and Ludwig moved to one side as the security man went to work. It was inevitable, Walton thought, that this would happen. FitzMaugham had been the living symbol of Popeek.

He walked to the battered door, reflecting that he would have it repaired at once. That thought led naturally to a new one, but before it was fully formed in his own mind, Ludwig voiced it.

"This is a terrible tragedy," the UN man said. "But one mitigating factor exists. I'm sure Mr. FitzMaugham's successor will be a fitting one. I'm confident you'll be able to carry on FitzMaugham's great work quite capably, Mr. Walton."

V

The new sign on the office door said:

ROY WALTON
Interim Director
Bureau of Population Equalization

He had argued against putting it up there, on the grounds that his appointment was strictly temporary, pending a meeting of the General Assembly to choose a new head for Popeek. But Ludwig had maintained it might be weeks or months before such a meeting could be held and that there was no harm in identifying his office.

"Everything under control?" the UN man asked.

Walton eyed him unhappily. "I guess so. Now all I have to do is start figuring out how Mr. FitzMaugham's filing system worked, and I'll be all set."

"You mean you don't know?"

"Mr. FitzMaugham took very few people into his confidence," Walton said. "Popeek was his special brain-child. He had lived with it so long he thought its workings were self-evident to everyone. There'll be a period of adjustment."

"Of course," Ludwig said.

"This conference you were going to have with the director yesterday when he—ah, what was it about?" Walton asked.

The UN man shrugged. "It's irrelevant now, I suppose. I wanted to find out how Popeek's subsidiary research lines were coming along. But I guess you'll have to go through Mr. FitzMaugham's files before you know anything, eh?" Ludwig stared at him sharply.

Suddenly, Walton did not like the cheerful UN man.

"There'll be a certain period of adjustment," he repeated. "I'll let you know when I'm ready to answer questions about Popeek."

"Of course. I didn't mean to imply any criticism of you or of the late director or of Popeek, Mr. Walton."

"Naturally. I understand, Mr. Ludwig."

Ludwig took his leave at last, and Walton was alone in the late Mr. FitzMaugham's office for the first time since the assassination. He spread his hands on the highly polished desk and twisted his wrists outward in a tense gesture. His fingers made squeaking sounds as they rubbed the wood surface.

It had been an uneasy afternoon yesterday, after the nightmare of the assassination and the subsequent security inquisition. Walton, wrung dry, had gone home early, leaving Popeek headless for two hours. The newsblares in the jetbus had been programmed with nothing but talk of the killing.

"A brutal hand today struck down the revered D. F. FitzMaugham, eighty-one, Director of Population Equalization. Security officials report definite prospects of solution of the shocking crime, and...."

The other riders in the bus had been vehemently outspoken.

"It's about time they let him have it," a fat woman in sleazy old clothes said. "That baby killer!"

"I knew they'd get him sooner or later," offered a thin, wispy-haired old man. "They *had* to."

"Rumor going around he was really a Herschelite...."

"Some new kid is taking over Popeek, they say. They'll get him too, mark my words."

Walton, huddling in his seat, pulled up his collar, and tried to shut his ears. It didn't work.

They'll get him too, mark my words.

He hadn't forgotten that prophecy by the time he reached his cubicle in upper Manhattan. The harsh words had drifted through his restless sleep all night.

Now, behind the safety of his office door, he thought of them again.

He couldn't hide. It hadn't worked for FitzMaugham, and it

wouldn't for him.

Hiding wasn't the answer. Walton smiled grimly. If martyrdom were in store for him, let martyrdom come. The work of Popeek had to go forward. He decided he would conduct as much of his official business as possible by screen; but when personal contact was necessary, he would make no attempt to avoid it.

He glanced around FitzMaugham's office. The director had been a product of the last century, and he had seen nothing ugly in the furnishings of the Cullen Building. Unlike Walton, then, he had not had his office remodeled.

That would be one of the first tasks—to replace the clumsy battery of tungsten-filament incandescents with a wall of electroluminescents, to replace the creaking sash windows with some decent opaquers, to get rid of the accursed gingerbread trimming that offended the eye in every direction. The *thunkety-thunk* air-conditioner would have to go too; he'd have a molecusorter installed in a day or two.

The redecorating problems were the minor ones. It was the task of filling FitzMaugham's giant shoes, even on an interim basis, that staggered Walton.

He fumbled in the desk for a pad and stylus. This was going to call for an agenda. Hastily he wrote:

1.	*Cancel*	*F's*		*appointments*
2.	*Investigate*	*setup*	*in*	*Files*
a)	*Lang*	*terraforming*		*project*
b)				*faster-than-light*
c)				*budget—stretchable?*
d)	*locate* *spy*	*pickups*	*in*	*building*
3.	*Meeting*	*with*	*section*	*chiefs*
4.	*Press* *conference*	*with*	*telefax*	*services*
5.	*See* *Ludwig* ...	*straighten*	*things*	*out*

6. Redecorate office

He thought for a moment, then erased a few of his numbers and changed*Press conference* to *6.* and *Redecorate office* to *4.* He licked the stylus and wrote in at the very top of the paper:

0. Finish Prior affair.

In a way, FitzMaugham's assassination had taken Walton off the hook on the Prior case. Whatever FitzMaugham suspected about Walton's activities yesterday morning no longer need trouble him. If the director had jotted down a memorandum on the subject, Walton would be able to find and destroy it when he went through FitzMaugham's files later. And if the dead man had merely kept the matter in his head, well, then it was safely at rest in the crematorium.

Walton groped in his jacket pocket and found the note his brother had slipped to him at lunchtime the day before. In the rush of events, Walton had not had a chance to destroy it.

Now, he read it once more, ripped it in half, ripped it again, and fed one quarter of the note into the disposal chute. He would get rid of the rest at fifteen-minute intervals, and he would defy anyone monitoring the disposal units to locate all four fragments.

Actually, he realized he was being overcautious. This was Director FitzMaugham's office and FitzMaugham's disposal chute. The director wouldn't have arranged to have his *own* chute monitored, would he?

Or would he? There was never any telling, with FitzMaugham. The old man had been terribly devious in every maneuver he made.

The room had the dry, crisp smell of the detecting devices that had been used—the close-to-the-ground, ugly metering-robots that had crawled all over the floor, sniffing up footprints and stray dandruff flakes for analysis, the chemical cleansers that had mopped the blood out of the rug. Walton cursed at the air-conditioner that was so inefficiently removing these smells from the air.

The annunciator chimed. Walton waited impatiently for a voice, then remembered that FitzMaugham had doggedly required an acknowledgment. He opened the channel and said, "This is Walton. In the future no acknowledgment will be necessary."

"Yes, sir. There's a reporter from *Citizen* here, and one from Globe Telefax."

"Tell them I'm not seeing anyone today. Here, I'll give them a statement. Tell them the Gargantuan task of picking up the reins where the late, great Director FitzMaugham dropped them is one that will require my full energy for the next several days. I'll be happy to hold my first official press conference as soon as Popeek is once again moving on an even keel. Got that?"

"Yes, sir."

"Good. Make sure they print it. And—oh, listen. If anyone shows up today or tomorrow who had an appointment with Director FitzMaugham, tell him approximately the same thing. Not in those flowery words, of course, but give him the gist of it. I've got a lot of catching up to do before I can see people."

"Certainly, Director Walton."

He grinned at the sound of those words, *Director Walton*. Turning away from the annunciator, he took out his agenda and checked off number one, *Cancel FitzMaugham's appointments*.

Frowning, he realized he had better add a seventh item to the list: *Appoint new assistant administrator*. Someone would have to handle his old job.

But now, top priority went to the item ticketed zero on the list: *Finish Prior affair*. He'd never be in a better position to erase the evidence of yesterday's illegality than he was right now.

"Connect me with euthanasia files, please."

A moment later a dry voice said, "Files."

"Files, this is Acting Director Walton. I'd like a complete transcript of your computer's activities for yesterday morning between 0900 and 1200, with each separate activity itemized. How soon can I have it?"

"Within minutes, Director Walton."

"Good. Send it sealed, by closed circuit. There's some top-level stuff on that transcript. If the seal's not intact when it gets here, I'll shake up the whole department."

"Yes, sir. Anything else, sir?"

"No, that'll be—on second thought, yes. Send up a list of all doctors who were examining babies in the clinic yesterday morning."

He waited. While he waited, he went through the top layer of memoranda in FitzMaugham's desk.

There was a note on top which read, *Appointment with Lamarre, 11 June—1215. Must be firm with him, and must handle with great delicacy. Perhaps time to let Walton know.*

Hmm, that was interesting, Walton thought. He had no idea who Lamarre might be, but FitzMaugham had drawn a spidery little star in the upper-right-hand corner of the memo sheet, indicating crash priority.

He flipped on the annunciator. "There's a Mr. Lamarre who had an appointment with Director FitzMaugham for 1215 today. If he calls, tell him I can't see him today but will honor the appointment tomorrow at the same time. If he shows up, tell him the same thing."

His watch said it was time to dispose of another fragment of Fred's message. He stuffed it into the disposal chute.

A moment later the green light flashed over the arrival bin; FitzMaugham had not been subject, as Walton had been in his previous office, to cascades of material arriving without warning.

Walton drew a sealed packet from the bin. He examined the seal and found it untampered, which was good; it meant the packet had come straight from the computer, and had not even been read by the technician in charge. With it was a typed list of five names—the doctors who had been in the lab the day before.

Breaking open the packet, Walton discovered seven closely-typed sheets with a series of itemized actions on them. He ran through them quickly, discarding sheets one, two, and three, which dealt with routine activities of the computer in the early hours of the previous day.

Item seventy-three was his request for Philip Prior's record card. He checked that one off.

Item seventy-four was his requisition for the key to the clinic's gene-sorting code.

Item seventy-five was his revision of Philip Prior's records, omitting all reference to his tubercular condition and to the euthanasia recommendation. Item seventy-six was the acknowledgment of this revision.

Item seventy-seven was his request for the boy's record card—this time, the amended one. The five items were dated and timed; the earliest was 1025, the latest 1037, all on June tenth.

Walton bracketed the five items thoughtfully, and scanned the rest of the page. Nothing of interest there, just more routine business. But item ninety-two, timed at 1102, was an intriguing one:

92: Full transcript of morning's transactions issued at request of Dr. Frederic Walton, 932K104AZ.

Fred hadn't been bluffing, then; he actually had possession of all the damning evidence. But when one dealt with a computer and with Donnerson micro-memory-tubes, the past was an extremely fluid entity.

"I want a direct line to the computer on floor twenty," he said.

After a brief lag a technician appeared on the screen. It was the same one he had spoken to earlier.

"There's been an error in the records," Walton said. "An error I wouldn't want to perpetuate. Will you set me up so I can feed a direct order into the machine?"

"Certainly, sir. Go ahead, sir."

"This is top secret. Vanish."

The technician vanished. Walton said, "Items seventy-three through seventy-seven on yesterday morning's record tape are to be deleted, and the information carried in those tubes is to be deleted as well. Furthermore, there is to be no record made of this transaction."

The voicewrite on floor twenty clattered briefly, and the order funneled into the computer. Walton waited a moment, tensely. Then he said, "All right, technician. Come back in where I can see you."

The technician appeared. Walton said, "I'm running a check now. Have the machine prepare another transcript of yesterday's activities between 0900 and 1200, and also one of today's doings for the last fifteen minutes."

"Right away, sir."

While he waited for the new transcripts to arrive, Walton studied the list of names on his desk. Five doctors—Gunther, Raymond, Archer, Hsi, Rein. He didn't know which one of them had examined the Prior baby, nor did he care to find out. All five would have to be transferred.

Meticulously, he took up his stylus and pad again, and plotted a destination for each:

Gunther ... *Zurich.*
Raymond ... *Glasgow.*
Archer ... *Tierra del Fuego.*
Hsi ... *Leopoldville.*
Rein ... Bangkok.

He nodded. That was optimum dissemination; he would put through notice of the transfers later in the day, and by nightfall the men would be on their way to their new scenes of operation. Perhaps they would never understand why they had been uprooted and sent away from New York.

The new transcripts arrived. Impatiently Walton checked through them.

In the June tenth transcript, item seventy-one dealt with smallpox statistics for North America 1822-68, and item seventy-two with the tally of antihistamine supply for requisitions for Clinic Three. There was no sign of any of Walton's requests. They had vanished from the record as completely as if they had never been.

Walton searched carefully through the June eleventh transcript for any mention of his deletion order. No, that hadn't been recorded either.

He smiled, his first honest smile since FitzMaugham's assassination. Now, with the computer records erased, the director dead, and the doctors on their way elsewhere, only Fred stood in the way of Roy's chance of escaping punishment for the Prior business.

He decided he'd have to take his chances with Fred. Perhaps brotherly love would seal his lips after all.

VI

The late Director FitzMaugham's files were spread over four floors of the building, but for Walton's purposes the only ones that mattered were those to which access was gained through the director's office alone.

A keyboard and screen were set into the wall to the left of the desk. Walton let his fingers rest lightly on the gleaming keys.

The main problem facing him, he thought, lay in not knowing where to begin. Despite his careful agenda, despite the necessary marshaling of his thoughts, he was still confused by the enormity of his job. The seven billion people of the world were in his hands. He could transfer fifty thousand New Yorkers to the bleak northern provinces of underpopulated Canada with the same quick ease that he had shifted five unsuspecting doctors half an hour before.

After a few moments of uneasy thought he pecked out the short message, *Request complete data file on terraforming project.*

On the screen appeared the words, *Acknowledged and coded; prepare to receive.*

The arrival bin thrummed with activity. Walton hastily scooped out a double handful of typed sheets to make room for more. He grinned in anguish as the paper kept on coming. FitzMaugham's files on terraforming, no doubt, covered reams and reams.

Staggering, he carted it all over to his desk and began to skim through it. The data began thirty years earlier, in 2202, with a photostat of a letter from Dr. Herbert Lang to FitzMaugham, proposing a project whereby the inner planets of the solar system could be made habitable by human beings.

Appended to that was FitzMaugham's skeptical, slightly mocking reply; the old man had kept everything, it seemed, even letters which showed him in a bad light.

After that came more letters from Lang, urging FitzMaugham to plead terraforming's case before the United States Senate, and FitzMaugham's increasingly more enthusiastic answers. Finally, in 2212, a notation that the Senate had voted a million-dollar appropriation to Lang—a miniscule amount, in terms of the overall need, but it was enough to cover preliminary research. Lang had been grateful.

Walton skimmed through more-or-less familiar documents on the nature of the terraforming project. He could study those in detail later, if time permitted. What he wanted now was information on the current status of the project; FitzMaugham had been remarkably silent about it, though the public impression had been created that a team of engineers headed by Lang was already at work on Venus.

He shoved whole handfuls of letters to one side, looking for those of recent date.

Here was one dated 1 Feb 2232, FitzMaugham to Lang: it informed the scientist that passage of the Equalization Act was imminent, and that Lang stood to get a substantial appropriation from the UN in that event. A jubilant reply from Lang was attached.

Following that came another, 10 May 2232, FitzMaugham to Lang: official authorization of Lang as an executive member of Popeek, and appropriation of—Walton's eyes bugged—five billion dollars for terraforming research.

Note from Lang to FitzMaugham, 14 May: the terraforming crew was leaving for Venus immediately.

Note from FitzMaugham to Lang, 16 May: best wishes, and Lang was instructed to contact FitzMaugham without fail at weekly intervals.

Spacegram from Lang to FitzMaugham, 28 May: arrived at Venus safely, preparing operation as scheduled.

The file ended there. Walton rummaged through the huge heap, hoping to discover a later communiqué; by FitzMaugham's own request, Lang should have contacted Popeek about four days ago with his first report.

Possibly it had gone astray in delivery, Walton thought. He spent twenty minutes digging through the assorted material before remembering that he could get a replacement within seconds from the filing computer.

He typed out a requisition for any and all correspondence between Director FitzMaugham and Dr. Herbert Lang that was dated after 28 May 2232.

The machine acknowledged, and a moment later replied, *This material is not included in memory banks.*

Walton frowned, gathered up most of his superfluous terraforming data, and deposited it in a file drawer. The status of the project, then, was uncertain: the terraformers were on Venus and presumably at work, but were yet to be heard from.

The next Popeek project to track down would be the faster-than-light spaceship drive. But after the mass of data Walton had just absorbed, he found himself hesitant to wade through another collection so soon.

He realized that he was hungry for the sight of another human being. He had spent the whole morning alone, speaking to anonymous underlings via screen or annunciator, and requisitioning material from an even more impersonal computer. He wanted noise, life, people around him.

He snapped on the annunciator. "I'm calling an immediate meeting of the Popeek section chiefs," he said. "In my office, in half an hour—at 1230 sharp. Tell them to drop whatever they're doing and come."

Just before they started to arrive, Walton felt a sudden sick wave of tension sweep dizzyingly over him. He pulled open the top drawer of his new desk and reached for his tranquilizer tablets. He suffered a moment of shock and disorientation before he realized that this was FitzMaugham's desk, not his own, and that FitzMaugham forswore all forms of sedation.

Chuckling nervously, Walton drew out his wallet and extracted the extra benzolurethrin he carried for just such emergencies. He popped the lozenge into his mouth only a moment before the spare figure of Lee Percy, first of the section chiefs to arrive, appeared in the screener outside the door.

"Roy? It's me—Percy."

"I can see you. Come on in, Lee."

Percy was in charge of public relations for Popeek. He was a tall, angular man with thick corrugated features.

After him came Teddy Schaunhaft, clinic coordinator; Pauline Medhurst, personnel director; Olaf Eglin, director of field agents; and Sue Llewellyn, Popeek's comptroller.

These five had constituted the central council of Popeek. Walton, as assistant administrator, had served as their coordinator, as well as handling population transfer and serving as a funnel for red tape. Above them all had been FitzMaugham, brooding over his charges like an untroubled Wotan; FitzMaugham had reserved for himself, aside from the task of general supervision, the special duties attendant on handling the terraforming and faster-than-light wings of Popeek.

"I should have called you together much earlier than this," Walton said when they were settled. "The shock, though, and the general confusion—"

"We understand, Roy," said Sue Llewellyn sympathetically. She was a chubby little woman in her fifties, whose private life was reported to be incredibly at variance with her pleasantly domestic appearance. "It's been rough on all of us, but you were so close to Mr. FitzMaugham...."

There was sympathetic clucking from various corners of the room. Walton said, "The period of mourning will have to be a brief one. What I'm suggesting is that business continue as usual, without a hitch." He glanced at Eglin, the director of field agents. "Olaf, is there a man in your section capable of handling your job?"

Eglin looked astonished for a moment, then mastered himself. "There must be five, at least. Walters, Lassen, Dominic—"

"Skip the catalogue," Walton told him. "Pick the man you think is best suited to replace you, and send his dossier up to me for approval."

"And where do *I* go?"

"You take over my slot as assistant administrator. As director of field agents, you're more familiar with the immediate problems of my old job than anyone else here."

Eglin preened himself smugly. Walton wondered if he had made an unwise choice; Eglin was competent enough, and would give forth one hundred percent effort at all times—but probably never the one hundred two percent a really great administrator could put out when necessary.

Still, the post had to be filled at once, and Eglin could pick up the reins faster than any of the others.

Walton looked around. "Otherwise, activities of Popeek will continue as under Mr. FitzMaugham, without a hitch. Any questions?"

Lee Percy raised an arm slowly. "Roy, I've got a problem I'd like to bring up here, as long as we're all together. There's a growing public sentiment that you and the late director were secretly Herschelites." He chuckled apologetically. "I know it sounds silly, but I just report what I hear."

"I'm familiar with the rumor," Walton said. "And I don't like it much, either. That's the sort of stuff riots are made of."

The Herschelites were extremists who advocated wholesale sterilization of defectives, mandatory birth control, and half a dozen other stringent remedies for overpopulation.

"What steps are you taking to counteract it?" Walton asked.

"Well," said Percy, "we're preparing a memorial program for FitzMaugham which will intimate that he was murdered by the Herschelites, who hated him."

"Good. What's the slant?"

"That he was too easygoing, too humane. We build up the Herschelites as ultrareactionaries who intend to enforce their will on humanity if they get the chance, and imply FitzMaugham was fighting them tooth and nail. We close the show with some shots of you picking up the great man's mantle, etcetera, etcetera. And a short speech from you affirming the basically humanitarian aims of Popeek."

Walton smiled approvingly and said, "I like it. When do you want me to do the speech?"

"We won't need you," Percy told him. "We've got plenty of stock footage, and we can whip the speech out of some spare syllables you left around."

Walton frowned. Too many of the public speeches of the day were synthetic, created by skilled engineers who split words into their component phonemes and reassembled them in any shape they pleased. "Let me check through my speech before you put it over, at least."

"Will do. And we'll squash this Herschelite thing right off the bat."

Pauline Medhurst squirmed uneasily in her chair. Walton caught the hint and recognized her.

"Uh, Roy, I don't know if this is the time or the place, but I got that transfer order of yours, the five doctors...."

"You did? Good," Walton said hurriedly. "Have you notified them yet?"

"Yes. They seemed unhappy about it."

"Refer them to FitzMaugham's book. Tell them they're cogs in a mighty machine, working to save humanity. We can't let personal considerations interefere, Pauline."

"If you could only explain why—"

"Yeah," interjected Schaunhaft, the clinic coordinator suddenly. "You cleaned out my whole morning lab shift down there. I was wondering—"

Walton felt like a stag at bay. "Look," he said firmly, cutting through the hubbub, "*I* made the transfer. I had reasons for doing it. It's your job to get the five men out where they've been assigned, and to get five new men in here at once. You're not required to make explanations to them—nor I to you."

Sudden silence fell over the office. Walton hoped he had not been too forceful, and cast suspicion on his actions by his stiffness.

"Whew!" Sue Llewellyn said. "You really mean business!"

"I said we were going to run Popeek without a hitch," Walton replied. "Just because you know my first name, that doesn't mean I'm not going to be as strong a director as FitzMaugham was."

Until the UN picks my successor, his mind added. Out loud he said, "Unless you have any further questions, I'll ask you now to return to your respective sections."

He sat slumped at his desk after they were gone, trying to draw on some inner reserve of energy for the strength to go on.

One day at the job, and he was tired, terribly tired. And it would be six weeks or more before the United Nations convened to choose the next director of Popeek.

He didn't know who that man would be. He expected they would offer the job to him, provided he did competent work during the interim; but, wearily, he saw he would have to turn the offer down.

It was not only that his nerves couldn't handle the grinding daily tension of the job; he saw now what Fred might be up to, and it stung.

What if his brother were to hold off exposing him until the moment the UN proffered its appointment ... and then took that moment to reveal that the head of Popeek, far from being an iron-minded Herschelite, had actually been guilty of an irregularity that transgressed against one of Popeek's own operations? He'd be finished. He'd be laughed out of public life for good—and probably prosecuted in the bargain—if Fred exposed him.

And Fred was perfectly capable of doing just that.

Walton saw himself spinning dizzily between conflicting alternatives. Keep the job and face his brother's exposé? Or resign, and vanish into anonymity. Neither choice seemed too appealing.

Shrugging, he dragged himself out of his chair, determined to shroud his conflict behind the mask of work. He typed a request to Files, requisitioning data on the faster-than-light project.

Moments later, the torrent began—rising from somewhere in the depths of the giant computer, rumbling upward through the conveyor system, moving onward toward the twenty-ninth floor and the office of Interim Director Walton.

VII

The next morning there was a crowd gathered before the Cullen Building when Walton arrived.

There must have been at least a hundred people, fanning outward from a central focus. Walton stepped from the jetbus and, with collar pulled up carefully to obscure as much of his face as possible, went to investigate.

A small red-faced man stood on a rickety chair against the side of the building. He was flanked by a pair of brass flagpoles, one bearing the American flag and the other the ensign of the United Nations. His voice was a biting rasp—probably, thought Walton, intensified, sharpened, and made more irritating by a harmonic modulator at his throat. An irritating voice put its message across twice as fast as a pleasant one.

He was shouting, "This is the place! Up here, in this building, that's where they are! That's where Popeek wastes our money!"

From the slant of the man's words Walton instantly thought: *Herschelite!*

He repressed his anger and, for once, decided to stay and hear the extremist out. He had never really paid much attention to Herschelite propaganda—he had been exposed to little of it—and he realized that now, as head of Popeek, he owed it to himself to become familiar with the anti-Popeek arguments of both extremist factions—those who insisted Popeek was a tyranny, and the Herschelites, who thought it was too weak.

"This Popeek," the little man said, accenting the awkwardness of the word. "You know what it is? It's a stopgap. It's a silly, soft-minded, half-hearted attempt at solving our problems. It's a fake, a fraud, a phony!"

There was real passion behind the words. Walton distrusted small men with deep wells of passion; he no more enjoyed their company than he did that of a dynamo or an atomic pile. They were always threatening to explode.

The crowd was stirring restlessly. The Herschelite was getting to them, one way or another. Walton drew back nervously, not wanting to be recognized, and stationed himself at the fringe of the crowd.

"Some of you don't like Popeek for this reason or that reason. But let me tell you something, friends ... you're wronger than they are! We've got to get tough with ourselves! We have to face the truth! Popeek is an unrealistic half-solution to man's problems. Until we limit birth, establish rigid controls over who's going to live and who isn't, we—"

It was straight Herschelite propaganda, undiluted. Walton wasn't surprised when someone in the audience interrupted, growling, "And who's going to set those controls? You?"

"You trusted yourselves to Popeek, didn't you? Why hesitate, then, to trust yourselves to Abel Herschel and his group of workers for the betterment and purification of mankind?"

Walton was almost limp with amazement. The Herschelite group was so much more drastic in its approach than Popeek that he wondered how they dared come out with these views in public. Animosity was high enough against Popeek; would the public accept a group more stringent yet?

The little man's voice rose high. "Onward with the Herschelites! Mankind must move forward! The Equalization people represent the forces of decay and sloth!"

Walton turned to the man next to him and murmured, "But Herschel's a fanatic. They'll kill all of us in the name of mankind."

The man looked puzzled; then, accepting the idea, he nodded. "Yeah, buddy. You know, you may have something there."

That was all the spark needed. Walton edged away surreptitiously and watched it spread through the crowd, while the little man's harangue grew more and more inflammatory.

Until a rock arced through the air from somewhere, whipped across the billowing UN flag, and cracked into the side of the building. That was the signal.

A hundred men and women converged on the little man on the battered chair. "*We have to face the truth!*" the harsh voice cried; then the flags were swept down, trampled on. Flagpoles fell, ringing metallically on the concrete; the chair toppled. The little man was lost beneath a tide of remorseless feet and arms.

A siren screamed.

"Cops!" Walton yelled from his vantage point some thirty feet away, and abruptly the crowd melted away in all directions, leaving

Walton and the little man alone on the street. A security wagon drew up. Four men in gray uniforms sprang out.

"What's been going on here? Who's this man?" Then, seeing Walton, "Hey! Come over here!"

"Of course, officer." Walton turned his collar down and drew near. He spotted the glare of a ubiquitous video camera and faced it squarely. "I'm Director Walton of Popeek," he said loudly, into the camera. "I just arrived here a few minutes ago. I saw the whole thing."

"Tell us about it, Mr. Walton," the security man said.

"It was a Herschelite." Walton gestured at the broken body crumpled against the ground. "He was delivering an inflammatory speech aimed against Popeek, with special reference to the late Director FitzMaugham and myself. I was about to summon you and end the disturbance, when the listeners became aware that the man was a Herschelite. When they understood what he was advocating, they—well, you see the result."

"Thank you, sir. Terribly sorry we couldn't have prevented it. Must be very unpleasant, Mr. Walton."

"The man was asking for trouble," Walton said. "Popeek represents the minds and hearts of the world. Herschel and his people seek to overthrow this order. I can't condone violence of any sort, naturally, but"—he smiled into the camera—"Popeek is a sacred responsibility to me. Its enemies I must regard as blind and misguided people."

He turned and entered the building, feeling pleased with himself. That sequence would be shown globally on the next news screenings; every newsblare in the world would be reporting his words.

Lee Percy would be proud of him. Without benefit either of rehearsal or phonemic engineering, Walton had delivered a rousing speech and turned a grisly incident into a major propaganda instrument.

And more than that, Director FitzMaugham would have been proud of him.

But beneath the glow of pride, he was trembling. Yesterday he had saved a boy by a trifling alteration of his genetic record; today he had killed a man by sending a whispered accusation rustling through a mob.

Power. Popeek represented power, perhaps the greatest power in the world. That power would have to be channeled somehow, now that it had been unleashed.

The stack of papers relating to the superspeed space drive was still on his desk when he entered the office. He had had time yesterday to read through just some of the earliest; then, the pressure of routine had dragged him off to other duties.

Encouraged by FitzMaugham, the faster-than-light project had originated about a decade or so before. It stemmed from the fact that the ion-drive used for travel between planets had a top velocity, a limiting factor of about ninety thousand miles per second. At that rate, it would take some eighteen years for a scouting party to visit the closest star and report back ... not very efficient for a planet in a hurry to expand outward.

A group of scientists had set to work developing a subspace warp drive, one that would cut across the manifold of normal space and allow speeds above light velocity.

All the records were here: the preliminary trials, the budget allocations, the sketches and plans, the names of the researchers. Walton ploughed painstakingly through them, learning names, assimilating scientific data. It seemed that, while it was still in its early stages, FitzMaugham had nurtured the project along with money from his personal fortune.

For most of the morning Walton leafed through documents describing projected generators, types of hull material, specifications, speculations. It was nearly noon when he came across the neatly-typed note from Colonel Leslie McLeod, one of the military scientists in charge of the ultradrive project. Walton read it through once, gasped, and read it again.

It was dated 14 June 2231, almost one year ago. It read:

My dear Mr. FitzMaugham:

I'm sure it will gladden you to learn that we have at last achieved success in our endeavors. The X-72 passed its last tests splendidly, and we are ready to leave on the preliminary scouting flight at once.

McLeod

It was followed by a note from FitzMaugham to McLeod, dated 15 June:

Dr. McLeod:

All best wishes on your great adventure. I trust you'll be departing, as usual, from the Nairobi base within the next few days. Please let me hear from you before departure.

FitzM.

The file concluded with a final note from McLeod to the director, dated 19 June 2231:

My dear Mr. FitzMaugham:

The X-72 will leave Nairobi in eleven hours, bound outward, manned by a crew of sixteen, including myself. The men are all impatient for the departure. I must offer my hearty thanks for the help you have given us over the past years, without which we would never have reached this step.

Flight plans include visiting several of the nearer stars, with the intention of returning either as soon as we have discovered a habitable extrasolar world, or one year after departure, whichever first occurs.

Sincere good wishes, and may you have as much success when you plead your case before the United Nations as we have had here—though you'll forgive me for hoping that our work might make any population equalization program on Earth totally superfluous!

McLeod

Walton stared at the three notes for a moment, so shocked he was unable to react. So a faster-than-light drive was not merely a hoped-for dream, but an actuality—with the first scouting mission a year absent already!

He felt a new burst of admiration for FitzMaugham. What a marvelous old scoundrel he had been!

Faster-than-light achieved, and the terraforming group on Venus, and neither fact released to the public ... or even specifically given to FitzMaugham's own staff, his alleged confidants.

It had been shrewd of him, all right. He had made sure nothing could go wrong. If something happened to Lang and his crew on Venus—and it was quite possible, since word from them was a week overdue—it would be easy to say that the terraforming project was still in the planning stage. In the event of success, the excuse was that word of their progress had been withheld for "security reasons."

And the same would apply to the space drive; if McLeod and his men vanished into the nether regions of interstellar space and never returned, FitzMaugham would not have had to answer for the failure of a project which, as far as the public knew, was still in the planning stage. It was a double-edged sword with the director controlling both edges.

And now Walton was in charge. He hoped he would be able to

continue manipulations with an aplomb worthy of the late Director FitzMaugham.

The annunciator chimed. "Dr. Lamarre is here for his appointment with you, Mr. Walton."

Walton was caught off guard. His mind raced furiously. *Lamarre? Who the dickens—oh, that left-over appointment of FitzMaugham's.*

"Tell Dr. Lamarre I'll be glad to see him in just a few minutes, please. I'll buzz you when I'm ready."

Hurriedly he gathered up the space-flight documents and jammed them in a file drawer near the data on terraforming. He surveyed his office; it looked neat, presentable. Glancing around, he made sure no stray documents were visible, documents which might reveal the truth about the space drive.

"Send in Dr. Lamarre," he said.

Dr. Lamarre was a short, thin, pale individual, with an uncertain wave in his sandy hair and a slight stoop of his shoulders. He carried a large, black leather portfolio which seemed on the point of exploding.

"Mr. Walton?"

"That's right. You're Dr. Lamarre?"

The small man handed him an engraved business card.

T.   *ELLIOT*   *LAMARRE*
Gerontologist

Walton fingered the card uneasily and returned it to its owner. "Gerontologist? One who studies ways of increasing the human life-span?"

"Precisely."

Walton frowned. "I presume you've had some previous dealings with the late Director FitzMaugham?"

Lamarre gaped. "You mean he didn't *tell* you?"

"Director FitzMaugham shared very little information with his assistants, Dr. Lamarre. The suddenness of my elevation to this post gave me little time to explore his files. Would you mind filling me in on the background?"

"Of course." Lamarre crossed his legs and squinted myopically across the desk at Walton. "To be brief, Mr. FitzMaugham first heard of my work fourteen years ago. Since that time, he's supported my experiments with private grants of his own, public appropriations whenever possible, and lately with money supplied by Popeek.

Naturally, because of the nature of my work I've shunned publicity. I completed my final tests last week, and was to have seen the director yesterday. But—"

"I know. I was busy going through Mr. FitzMaugham's files when you called yesterday. I didn't have time to see anyone." Walton wished he had checked on this man Lamarre earlier. Apparently it was a private project of FitzMaugham's and of some importance.

"May I ask what this 'work' of yours consists of?"

"Certainly. Mr. FitzMaugham expressed a hope that someday man's life span might be infinitely extended. I'm happy to report that I have developed a simple technique which will provide just that." The little man smiled in self-satisfaction. "In short," he said, "what I have developed, in everyday terms, is immortality, Mr. Walton."

VIII

Walton was becoming hardened to astonishment; the further he excavated into the late director's affairs, the less susceptible he was to the visceral reaction of shock.

Still, this stunned him for a moment.

"Did you say you'd perfected this technique?" he asked slowly. "Or that it was still in the planning stage?"

Lamarre tapped the thick, glossy black portfolio. "In here. I've got it all." He seemed ready to burst with self-satisfaction.

Walton leaned back, spread his fingers against the surface of the desk, and wrinkled his forehead. "I've had this job since 1300 on the tenth, Mr. Lamarre. That's exactly two days ago, minus half an hour.

And in that time I don't think I've had less than ten major shocks and half a dozen minor ones."

"Sir?"

"What I'm getting at is this: just why did Director FitzMaugham sponsor this project of yours?"

Lamarre looked blank. "Because the director was a great humanitarian, of course. Because he felt that the human life was short, far too short, and he wished his fellow men to enjoy long life. What other reason should there be?"

"I know FitzMaugham was a great man ... I was his secretary for three years." (*Though he never said a word about you, Dr. Lamarre*, Walton thought.) "But to develop immortality at this stage of man's existence...." Walton shook his head. "Tell me about your work, Dr. Lamarre."

"It's difficult to sum up readily. I've fought degeneration of the body on the cellular level, and my tests show a successful outcome. Phagocyte stimulation combined with—the data's all here, Mr. Walton. I needn't run through it for you."

He began to hunt in the portfolio, fumbling for something. After a moment he extracted a folded quarto sheet, spread it out, and nudged it across the desk toward Walton.

The director glanced at the sheet; it was covered with chemical equations. "Spare me the technical details, Dr. Lamarre. Have you tested your treatment yet?"

"With the only test possible, the test of time. There are insects in my laboratories that have lived five years or more—veritable Methuselahs of their genera. Immortality is not something one can test in less than infinite time. But beneath the microscope, one can see the cells regenerating, one can see decay combated...."

Walton took a deep breath. "Are you aware, Dr. Lamarre, that for the benefit of humanity I really should have you shot at once?"

"*What?*"

Walton nearly burst out laughing; the man looked outrageously funny with that look of shocked incomprehension on his face. "Do you understand what immortality would do to Earth?" he asked. "With no other planet of the solar system habitable by man, and none of the stars within reach? Within a generation we'd be living ten to the square inch. We'd—"

"Director FitzMaugham was aware of these things," Lamarre

interrupted sharply. "He had no intention of administering my discovery wholesale to the populace. What's more, he was fully confident that a faster-than-light space drive would soon let us reach the planets, and that the terraforming engineers would succeed with their work on Venus."

"Those two factors are still unknowns in the equation," Walton said. "Neither has succeeded, as of now. And we can't possibly let word of your discovery get out until there are avenues to handle the overflow of population already on hand."

"So you propose—"

"To confiscate the notes you have with you, and to insist that you remain silent about this serum of yours until I give you permission to announce it."

"And if I refuse?"

Walton spread his hands. "Dr. Lamarre, I'm a reasonable man trying to do a very hard job. You're a scientist—and a sane one, I hope. I'd appreciate your cooperation. Bear with me a few weeks, and then perhaps the situation will change."

Awkward silence followed. Finally Lamarre said, "Very well. If you'll return my notes, I promise to keep silent until you give me permission to speak."

"That won't be enough. I'll need to keep the notes."

Lamarre sighed. "If you insist," he said.

When he was again alone, Walton stored the thick portfolio in a file drawer and stared at it quizzically.

FitzMaugham, he thought, *you were incredible!*

Lamarre's immortality serum, or whatever it was, was deadly. Whether it actually worked or not was irrelevant. If word ever escaped that an immortality drug existed, there would be rioting and death on a vast scale.

FitzMaugham had certainly seen that, and yet he had sublimely underwritten development of the serum, knowing that if terraforming and the ultradrive project should fail, Lamarre's project represented a major threat to civilization.

Well, Lamarre had knuckled under to Walton willingly enough. The problem now was to contact Lang on Venus and find out what was happening up there....

"Mr. Walton," said the annunciator. "There's a coded message arriving for Director FitzMaugham."

"Where from?"

"From space, sir. They say they have news, but they won't give it to anyone but Mr. FitzMaugham."

Walton cursed. "Where is this message being received?"

"Floor twenty-three, sir. Communications."

"Tell them I'll be right down," Walton snapped.

He caught a lift tube and arrived on the twenty-third floor moments later. No sooner had the tube door opened than he sprang out, dodging around a pair of startled technicians, and sprinted down the corridor toward communications.

Here throbbed the network that held the branches of Popeek together. From here the screens were powered, the annunciators were linked, the phones connected.

Walton pushed open a door marked *Communications Central* and confronted four busy engineers who were crowded around a complex receiving mechanism.

"Where's that space message?" he demanded of the sallow young engineer who approached him.

"Still coming in, sir. They're repeating it over and over. We're triangulating their position now. Somewhere near the orbit of Pluto, Mr. Walton."

"Devil with that. Where's the message?"

Someone handed him a slip of paper. It said, *Calling Earth. Urgent call, top urgency, crash urgency. Will communicate only with D. F. FitzMaugham.*

"This all it is?" Walton asked. "No signature, no ship name?"

"That's right, Mr. Walton."

"Okay. Find them in a hurry and send them a return message. Tell them FitzMaugham's dead and I'm his successor. Mention me by name."

"Yes, sir."

He stamped impatiently around the lab while they set to work beaming the message into the void. Space communication was a field that dazzled and bewildered Walton, and he watched in awe as they swung into operation.

Time passed. "You know of any ships supposed to be in that

sector?" he asked someone.

"No, sir. We weren't expecting any calls except from Lang on Venus—" The technician gasped, realizing he had made a slip, and turned pale.

"That's all right," Walton assured him. "I'm the director, remember? I know all about Lang."

"Of course, sir."

"Here's a reply, sir," another of the nameless, faceless technicians said. Walton scanned it.

It read, *Hello Walton. Request further identification before we report. McL.*

A little shudder of satisfaction shook Walton at the sight of the initialed *McL.* at the end of the message. That could mean only McLeod—and *that* could mean only one thing: the experimental starship had returned!

Walton realized depressedly that this probably implied that they hadn't found any Earth-type worlds among the stars. McLeod's note to FitzMaugham had said they would search for a year, and would return home at the end of that time if they had no success. And just about a year had elapsed.

He said, "Send this return message: McLeod, Nairobi, X-72. Congratulations! Walton."

The technician vanished again, leaving Walton alone. He gazed moodily at the complex maze of equipment all around him, listened to the steady *tick-tick* of the communication devices, strained his ears to pick up fragments of conversation from the men.

After what seemed like an hour, the technician returned. "There's a message coming through now, sir. We're decoding it as fast as we can."

"Make it snappy," Walton said. His watch read 1429. Only twenty minutes had passed since he had gone down there.

A grimy sheet of paper was thrust under his nose. He read it:

Hello Walton, this is McLeod. Happy to report that experimental ship X-72 is returning home with all hands in good shape, after a remarkable one-year cruise of the galaxy. I feel like Ulysses returning to Ithaca, except we didn't have such a hard time of it.

I imagine you'll be interested in this: we found a perfectly lovely and livable world in the Procyon system. No intelligent life at all, and incredibly fine climate. Pity old FitzMaugham couldn't have lived to hear about it. Be seeing you soon. McLeod.

Walton's hands were still shaking as he pressed the actuator that would let him back into his office. He would have to call another meeting of the section chiefs again, to discuss the best method of presenting this exciting news to the world.

For one thing, they would have to explain away FitzMaugham's failure to reveal that the X-72 had been sent out over a year ago. That could be easily handled.

Then, there would have to be a careful build-up: descriptions of the new world, profiles of the heroes who had found it, etcetera. Someone was going to have to work out a plan for emigration ... unless the resourceful FitzMaugham had already drawn up such a plan and stowed it in Files for just this anticipated day.

And then, perhaps Lamarre could be called back now, and allowed to release his discovery. Plans buzzed in Walton's mind: in the event that people proved reluctant to leave Earth and conquer an unknown world, no matter how tempting the climate, it might be feasible to dangle immortality before them—to restrict Lamarre's treatment to volunteer colonists, or something along that line. There was plenty of time to figure that out, Walton thought.

He stepped into his office and locked the door behind him. A glow of pleasure surrounded him; for once it seemed that things were heading in the right direction. He was happy, in a way, that FitzMaugham was no longer in charge. Now, with mankind on the threshold of—

Walton blinked. *Did I leave that file drawer open when I left the office?* he wondered. He was usually more cautious than that.

The file was definitely open now, as were the two cabinets adjoining it. Numbly he swung the cabinet doors wider, peered into the shadows, groped inside.

The drawers containing the documents pertaining to terraforming and to McLeod's space drive seemed intact. But the cabinet in which Walton had placed Lamarre's portfolio—that cabinet was totally empty!

Someone's been in here, he thought angrily. And then the anger changed to agony as he remembered what had been in Lamarre's portfolio, and what would happen if that formula were loosed indiscriminately in the world.

IX

The odd part of it, Walton thought, was that there was absolutely nothing he could do.

He could call Sellors and give him a roasting for not guarding his office properly, but that wouldn't restore the missing portfolio.

He could send out a general alarm, and thereby let the world know that there was such a thing as Lamarre's formula. That would be catastrophic.

Walton slammed the cabinet shut and spun the lock. Then, heavily, he dropped into his chair and rested his head in his arms. All the jubilation of a few moments before had suddenly melted into dull apprehension.

Suspects? Just two—Lamarre, and Fred. Lamarre because he was obvious; Fred because he was likely to do anything to hurt his brother.

"Give me Sellors in security," Walton said quietly.

Sellors' bland face appeared on the screen. He blinked at the sight of Walton, causing Walton to wonder just how ghastly his own appearance was; even with the executive filter touching up the transmitted image, sprucing him up and falsifying him for the public benefit, he probably looked dreadful.

"Sellors, I want you to send out a general order for a Dr. Lamarre. You'll find his appearance recorded on the entrance tapes for today; he came to see me earlier. The first name is—ah—Elliot. T. Elliot Lamarre, gerontologist. I don't know where he lives."

"What should I do when I find him, sir?"

"Bring him here at once. And if you catch him at home, slap a seal on his door. He may be in possession of some very important secret documents."

"Yes, sir."

"And get hold of the doorsmith who repaired my office door; I want the lock calibration changed at once."

"Certainly, sir."

The screen faded. Walton turned back to his desk and busied himself in meaningless paper work, trying to keep himself from thinking.

A few moments later the screen brightened again. It was Fred.

Walton stared coldly at his brother's image. "Well?"

Fred chuckled. "Why so pale and wan, dear brother? Disappointed in love?"

"What do you want?"

"An audience with His Highness the Interim Director, if it please His Grace." Fred grinned unpleasantly. "A private, audience, if you please, m'lord."

"Very well. Come on up here."

Fred shook his head. "Sorry, no go. There are too many tricky spy pickups in that office of yours. Let's meet elsewhere, shall we?"

"Where?"

"That club you belong to. The Bronze Room."

Walton sputtered. "But I can't leave the building now! There's no one who—"

"Now," Fred interrupted. "The Bronze Room. It's in the San Isidro, isn't it? Top of Neville Prospect?"

"All right," said Walton resignedly. "There's a doorsmith coming up here to do some work. Give me a minute to cancel the assignment and I'll meet you downstairs."

"You leave now," Fred said. "I'll arrive five minutes after you. And you won't need to cancel anything. *I* was the doorsmith."

Neville Prospect was the most fashionable avenue in all of New York City, a wide strip of ferroconcrete running up the West Side between Eleventh Avenue and the West Side Drive from Fortieth to Fiftieth Street. It was bordered on both sides by looming apartment buildings in which a man of wealth might have as many as four or five rooms to his suite; and at the very head of the Prospect, facing down-town, was the mighty San Isidro, a buttressed fortress of gleaming metal and stone whose mighty, beryllium-steel supports swept out in a massive arc five hundred feet in either direction.

On the hundred fiftieth floor of the San Isidro was the exclusive Bronze Room, from whose quartz windows might be seen all the sprawling busyness of Manhattan and the close-packed confusion of New Jersey just across the river.

The jetcopter delivered Walton to the landing-stage of the Bronze Room; he tipped the man too much and stepped within. A door of dull bronze confronted him. He touched his key to the signet plate; the door pivoted noiselessly inward, admitting him.

The color scheme today was gray: gray light streamed from the luminescent walls, gray carpets lay underfoot, gray tables with gray dishes were visible in the murky distance. A gray-clad waiter, hardly more than four feet tall, sidled up to Walton.

"Good to see you again, sir," he murmured. "You have not been here of late."

"No," Walton said. "I've been busy."

"A terrible tragedy, the death of Mr. FitzMaugham. He was one of our most esteemed members. Will you have your usual room today, sir?"

Walton shook his head. "I'm entertaining a guest—my brother, Fred. We'll need a compartment for two. He'll identify himself when he arrives."

"Of course. Come with me, please."

The gnome led him through a gray haze to another bronze door, down a corridor lined with antique works of art, through an interior room decorated with glowing lumi-facts of remarkable quality, past a broad quartz window so clean as to be dizzyingly invisible, and up to a narrow door with a bright red signet plate in its center.

"For you, sir."

Walton touched his key to the signet plate; the door crumpled like a fan. He stepped inside, gravely handed the gnome a bill, and closed the door.

The room was tastefully furnished, again in gray; the Bronze Room was always uniformly monochromatic, though the hue varied with the day and with the mood of the city. Walton had long speculated on what the club precincts would be like were the electronic magic disconnected.

Actually, he knew, none of the Bronze Room's appurtenances had any color except when the hand in the control room threw the switch. The club held many secrets. It was FitzMaugham who had brought about Walton's admission to the club, and Walton had been deeply grateful.

He was in a room just comfortably large enough for two, with a single bright window facing the Hudson, a small onyx table, a tiny screen tastefully set in the wall, and a bar. He dialed himself a filtered rum, his favorite drink. The dark, cloudy liquid came pouring instantly from the spigot.

The screen suddenly flashed a wave of green, breaking the ubiquitous grayness. The green gave way to the bald head and scowling face of Kroll, the Bronze Room's door-man.

"Sir, there is a man outside who claims to be your brother. He alleges he has an appointment with you here."

"That's right, Kroll; send him in. Fulks will bring him to my room."

"Just one moment, sir. First it is needful to verify." Kroll's face vanished and Fred's appeared.

"Is this the man?" Kroll's voice asked.

"Yes," Walton said. "You can send my brother in."

Fred seemed a little dazed by the opulence. He sat gingerly on the edge of the foamweb couch, obviously attempting to appear blasé and painfully conscious of his failure to do so.

"This is quite a place," he said finally.

Walton smiled. "A little on the palatial side for my tastes. I don't come here often. The transition hurts too much when I go back outside."

"FitzMaugham got you in here, didn't he?"

Walton nodded.

"I thought so," Fred said. "Well, maybe someday soon I'll be a member too. Then we can meet here more often. We don't see enough of each other, you know."

"Dial yourself a drink," Walton said. "Then tell me what's on your mind—or were you just angling to get an invite up here?"

"It was more than that. But let me get a drink before we begin."

Fred dialed a Weesuer, heavy on the absinthe, and took a few sampling sips before wheeling around to face Walton. He said, "One of the minor talents I acquired in the course of my wanderings was doorsmithing. It's really not very difficult to learn, for a man who applies himself."

"You were the one who repaired my office door?"

Fred smirked. "I was. I wore a mask, of course, and my uniform was borrowed. Masks are very handy things. They make them most convincingly, nowadays. As, for instance, the one worn by the man who posed as Ludwig."

"What do you know about—"

"*Nothing.* And that's the flat truth, Roy. I didn't kill FitzMaugham, and I don't know who did." He drained his drink and dialed another. "No, the old man's death is as much of a mystery to me as it is to you. But I have to thank you for wrecking the door so completely when you blasted your way in. It gave me a chance to make some repairs when I most wanted to."

Walton held himself very carefully in check. He knew exactly what Fred was going to say in the next few minutes, but he refused to let himself precipitate the conversation.

With studied care he rose, dialed another filtered rum for himself, and gently slid the initiator switch on the electroluminescent kaleidoscope embedded in the rear wall.

A pattern of lights sprang into being—yellow, pale rose, blue, soft green. They wove together, intertwined, sprang apart into a sharp hexagon, broke into a scatter-pattern, melted, seemed to fall to the carpet in bright flakes.

"Shut that thing off!" Fred snapped suddenly. "Come on! Shut it! *Shut it!*"

Walton swung around. His brother was leaning forward intently, eyes clamped tight shut. "Is it off?" Fred asked. "Tell me!"

Shrugging, Walton canceled the signal and the lights faded. "You can open your eyes, now. It's off."

Cautiously Fred opened his eyes. "None of your fancy tricks, Roy!"

"Trick?" Walton asked innocently. "What trick? Simple decoration, that's all—and quite lovely, too. Just like the kaleidowhirls you've seen on video."

Fred shook his head. "It's not the same thing. How do I know it's not some sort of hypnoscreen? How do I know what those lights can do?"

Walton realized his brother was unfamiliar with wall kaleidoscopes. "It's perfectly harmless," he said. "But if you don't want it on, we can do without it."

"Good. That's the way I like it."

Walton observed that Fred's cool confidence seemed somewhat shaken. His brother had made a tactical error in insisting on holding their interview here, where Walton had so much the upper hand.

"May I ask again why you wanted to see me?" Walton said.

"There are those people," Fred said slowly, "who oppose the entire principle of population equalization."

"I'm aware of that. Some of them are members of this very club."

"Exactly. Some of them are. The ones I mean are the gentry, those still lucky enough to cling to land and home. The squire with a hundred acres in the Matto Grosso; the wealthy landowner of Liberia; the gentleman who controls the rubber output of one of the lesser Indonesian islands. These people, Roy, are unhappy over equalization. They know that sooner or later you and your Bureau will find out about them and will equalize them ... say, by installing a hundred Chinese on a private estate, or by using a private river for a nuclear turbine. You'll have to admit that their dislike of equalization is understandable."

"Everyone's dislike of equalization is understandable," Walton said. "I dislike it myself. You got your evidence of that two days ago. No one likes to give up special privileges."

"You see my point, then. There are perhaps a hundred of these men in close contact with each other—"

"*What!*"

"Ah, yes," Fred said. "A league. A conspiracy, it might almost be called. Very, very shady doings."

"Yes."

"I work for them," Fred said.

Walton let that soak in. "You're an employee of Popeek," he said. "Are you inferring that you're both an employee of Popeek and an employee of a group that seeks to undermine Popeek?"

Fred grinned proudly. "That's the position on the nose. It calls for remarkable compartmentalization of mind. I think I manage nicely."

Incredulously Walton said, "How long has this been going on?"

"Ever since I came to Popeek. This group is older than Popeek. They fought equalization all the way, and lost. Now they're working from the bottom up and trying to wreck things before you catch wise and confiscate their estates, as you're now legally entitled to do."

"And now that you've warned me they exist," Walton said, "you can be assured that that's the first thing I'll do. The second thing I'll do will be to have the security men track down their names and find out if there was an actual conspiracy. If there was, it's jail for them. And the third thing I'll do is discharge you from Popeek."

Fred shook his head. "You won't do any of those things, Roy. You can't."

"Why?"

"I know something about you that wouldn't look good if it came out in the open. Something that would get you bounced out of your high position in a flash."

"Not fast enough to stop me from setting the wheels going. My successor would continue the job of rooting out your league of landed gentry."

"I doubt that," Fred said calmly. "I doubt it very much— because *I'm* going to be your successor."

X

Crosscurrents of fear ran through Walton. He said, "What are you talking about?"

Fred folded his arms complacently. "I don't think it comes as news to you that I broke into your office this morning while you were out. It was very simple: when I installed the lock, I built in a canceling circuit that would let me walk in whenever I pleased. And this morning I pleased. I was hoping to find something I could use as immediate leverage against you, but I hadn't expected anything as explosive as the portfolio in the left-hand cabinet.

"Where is it?"

Fred grinned sharply. "The contents of that portfolio are now in very safe keeping, Roy. Don't bluster and don't threaten, because it won't work. I took precautions."

"And—"

"And you know as well as I what would happen if that immortality serum got distributed to the good old man in the street," Fred said. "For one thing, there'd be a glorious panic. That would solve your population problem for a while, with millions killed in the rush. But after that—where would you equalize, with every man and woman on Earth living forever, and producing immortal children?"

"We don't know the long-range effects yet—"

"Don't temporize. You damned well know it'd be the biggest upheaval the world has ever seen." Fred paused. "My employers," he said, "are in possession of the Lamarre formulas now."

"And with great glee are busy making themselves immortals."

"No. They don't trust the stuff, and won't use it until it's been tried on two or three billion guinea pigs. Human ones."

"They're not planning to release the serum, are they?" Walton gasped.

"Not immediately," Fred said. "In exchange for certain concessions on your part, they're prepared to return Lamarre's portfolio to you without making use of it."

"Concessions? Such as what?"

"That you refrain from declaring their private lands open territory for equalization. That you resign your post as interim director. That you go before the General Assembly and recommend me as your successor."

"*You?*"

"Who else is best fitted to serve the interests I represent?"

Walton leaned back, his face showing a mirth he scarcely felt. "Very neat, Fred. But full of holes. First thing, what assurance have I that your wealthy friends won't keep a copy of the Lamarre formula and use it as a bludgeon in the future against anyone they don't agree with?"

"None," Fred admitted.

"Naturally. What's more, suppose I refuse to give in and your employers release the serum to all and sundry. Who gets hurt? Not me; I live in a one-room box myself. But they'll be filling the world with billions and billions of people. Their beloved estates will be overrun by the hungry multitudes, whether they like it or not. And no fence will keep out a million hungry people."

"This is a risk they recognize," Fred said.

Walton smiled triumphantly. "You mean they're bluffing! They know they don't dare release that serum, and they think they can get me out of the way and you, their puppet, into office by making menacing noises. All right. I'll call their bluff."

"You mean you refuse?"

"Yes," Walton said. "I have no intention of resigning my interim directorship, and when the Assembly convenes I'm going to ask for the job on a permanent basis. They'll give it to me."

"And my evidence against you? The Prior baby?"

"Hearsay. Propaganda. I'll laugh it right out of sight."

"Try laughing off the serum, Roy. It won't be so easy as all that."

"I'll manage," Walton said tightly. He crossed the room and jabbed down on the communicator stud. The screen lit; the wizened face of the tiny servitor appeared.

"Sir?"

"Fulks, would you show this gentleman out of my chamber, please? He has no further wish to remain with me."

"Right away, Mr. Walton."

"Before you throw me out," Fred said, "let me tell you one more thing."

"Go ahead."

"You're acting stupidly—though that's nothing new for you, Roy. I'll give you a week's grace to make up your mind. Then the serum goes into production."

"My mind is made up," Walton said stiffly. The door telescoped and Fulks stood outside. He smiled obsequiously at Walton, bowed to Fred, and said to him, "Would you come with me, please?"

It was like one of those dreams, Walton thought, in which you were a butler bringing dishes to the table, and the tray becomes obstinately stuck to your fingertips and refuses to be separated; or in which the Cavendishes are dining in state and you come to the table nude; or in which you float downward perpetually with never a sign of bottom.

There never seemed to be any way out. Force opposed force and he seemed doomed always to be caught in the middle.

Angrily he snapped the kaleidoscope back on and let its everchanging swirl of color distract him. But in the depth of the deepest violet he kept seeing his brother's mocking face.

He summoned Fulks.

The gnome looked up at him expectantly. "Get me a jetcopter," Walton ordered. "I'll be waiting on the west stage for it."

"Very good, sir."

Fulks never had any problems, Walton reflected sourly. The little man had found his niche in life; he spent his days in the plush comfort of the Bronze Room, seeing to the wants of the members. Never any choices to make, never any of the agonizing decisions that complicated life.

Decisions. Walton realized that one particular decision had been made for him, that of seeking the directorship permanently. He had not been planning to do that. Now he had no choice but to remain in office as long as he could.

He stepped out onto the landing stage and into the waiting jetcopter. "Cullen Building," he told the robopilot abstractedly.

He did not feel very cheerful.

The annunciator panel in Walton's office was bright as a Christmas tree; the signal bulbs were all alight, each representing someone anxious to speak to him. He flipped over the circuit-breaker, indicating he was back in his office, and received the first call.

It was from Lee Percy. Percy's thick features were wrinkled into a smile. "Just heard that speech you made outside the building this morning, Roy. It's getting a big blare on the newsscreens. Beautiful! Simply beautiful! Couldn't have been better if we'd concocted it ourselves."

"Glad you like it," Walton said. "It really was off the cuff."

"Even better, then. You're positively a genius. Say, I wanted to tell you that we've got the FitzMaugham memorial all whipped up and ready to go. Full channel blast tonight over all media at 2000 sharp ... a solid hour block. Nifty. Neat."

"Is my speech in the program?"

"Sure is, Roy. A slick one, too. Makes two speeches of yours blasted in a single day."

"Send me a transcript of my speech before it goes on the air," Walton said. "I want to read and approve that thing if it's supposed to be coming out of my mouth."

"It's a natural, Roy. You don't have to worry."

"*I want to read it beforehand!*" Walton snapped.

"Okay, okay. Don't chew my ears off. I'll ship it to you posthaste, man. Ease up. Pop a pill. You aren't loose, Roy."

"I can't afford to be," Walton said.

He broke contact and almost instantly the next call blossomed on the screen. Walton recognized the man as one of the technicians from communications, floor twenty-three.

"Well?"

"We heard from McLeod again, sir. Message came in half an hour ago and we've been trying to reach you ever since."

"I wasn't in. Give me the message."

The technician unfolded a slip of paper. "It says, 'Arriving Nairobi tonight, will be in New York by morning. McLeod.'"

"Good. Send him confirmation and tell him I'll keep the entire morning free to see him."

"Yes, sir."

"Oh—anything from Venus?"

The technician shook his head emphatically. "Not a peep. We can't make contact with Dr. Lang at all."

Walton frowned. He wondered what was happening to the terraforming crew up there. "Keep trying, will you? Work a twenty-four-hour-a-day schedule. Draw extra pay. But get in touch with Lang, dammit!"

"Y-yes, sir. Anything else?"

"No. Get off the line."

As the contact snapped Walton smoothly broke connection again, leaving ten more would-be callers sputtering. A row of lights a foot long indicated their presence on the line. Walton ignored them and turned instead to his newsscreen.

The 1400 news was on. He fiddled with the controls and saw his own face take form on the screen. He was standing outside the Cullen Building, looking right out of the screen at himself, and in the background could be seen a huddled form under a coat. The dead Herschelite.

Walton of the screen was saying, "... The man was asking for trouble. Popeek represents the minds and hearts of the world. Herschel and his people seek to overthrow this order. I can't condone violence of any sort, naturally, but Popeek is a sacred responsibility to me. Its enemies I must regard as blind and misguided people."

He was smiling into the camera, but there was something behind the smile, something cold and steely, that astonished the watching Walton. *My God*, he thought. *Is that genuine? Have I really grown so hard?*

Apparently he had. He watched himself turn majestically and stride into the Cullen Building, stronghold of Popeek. There was definitely a commanding air about him.

The commentator was saying, "With those heartfelt words, Director Walton goes to his desk in the Cullen Building to carry out his weighty task. To bring life out of death, joy out of sadness—this is the job facing Popeek, and this is the sort of man to whom it has been entrusted. Roy Walton, we salute you!"

The screen panned to a still of Director FitzMaugham. "Meanwhile," the commentator went on, "Walton's predecessor, the late D. F. FitzMaugham, went to his rest today. Police are still hoping to uncover the group responsible for his brutal slaying, and report a good probability of success. Tonight all channels will carry a memorial program for this great leader of humanity. D. F. FitzMaugham, hail and farewell!"

A little sickened, Walton snapped the set off. He had to admire Lee Percy; the propaganda man had done his job well. With a minor assist from Walton by way of a spontaneous speech, Percy had contrived to gain vast quantities of precious air time for Popeek. All to the good.

The annunciator was still blinking violently; it seemed about to explode with the weight of pent-up, frustrated calls. Walton nudged a red stud at the top and Security Chief Sellors entered the screen.

"Sellors, sir. We've been looking for this Lamarre. Can't find him anywhere."

"What?"

"We checked him to his home. He got there, all right. Then he disappeared. No sign of him anywhere in the city. What now, sir?"

Walton felt his fingers quivering. "Order a tracer sent out through all of Appalachia. No, cancel that—make it country-wide. Beam his description everywhere. Got any snaps?"

"Yes, sir."

"Get them on the air. Tell the country this man is vital to global security. Find him, Sellors."

"We'll give it a try."

"Better than that. You'll *find* him. If he doesn't turn up within eight hours, shift the tracer to world-wide. He might be anywhere—and he has to be found!"

Walton blanked the screen and avoided the next caller. He called his secretary and said, "Will you instruct everyone now calling me to refer their business downstairs to Assistant Administrator Eglin. If they don't want to do that, tell them to put it in writing and send it to me. I can't accept any more calls just now." Then he added, "Oh, put me through to Eglin myself before you let any of those calls reach him."

———————————

Eglin's face appeared on the private screen that linked the two offices. The small man looked dark-browed and harried. "This is a hell of a job, Roy," he sighed.

"So is mine," Walton said. "Look, I've got a ton of calls on the wire, and I'm transferring them all down to you. Throw as many as you can down to the subordinates. It's the only way to keep your sanity."

"Thanks. Thanks loads, Roy. All I need now is some more calls."

"Can't be helped. Who'd you pick for your replacement as director of field agents?" Walton asked.

"Lassen. I sent his dossier to you hours ago."

"Haven't read it yet. Is he on the job already?"

"Sure. He's been there since I moved up here," Eglin said. "What—"

"Never mind," said Walton. He hung up and called Lassen, the new director of field agents.

Lassen was a boyish-looking young man with stiff sandy hair and a sternly efficient manner. Walton said, "Lassen, I want you to do a job for me. Get one of your men to make up a list of the hundred biggest private estates still unequalized. I want the names of their owners, location of the estates, acreage, and things like that. Got it?"

"Right. When will you want it, Mr. Walton?"

"Immediately. But I don't want it to be a sloppy job. This is top important, double."

Lassen nodded. Walton grinned at him—the boy seemed to be in good control of himself—and clicked off.

He realized that he'd been engaged in half a dozen high-power conversations without a break, over a span of perhaps twenty minutes. His heart was pounding; his feet felt numb.

He popped a benzolurethrin into his mouth and kept on going. He would need to act fast, now that the wheels were turning. McLeod arriving the next day to report the results of the faster-than-light expedition, Lamarre missing, Fred at large and working for a conspiracy of landowners—Walton foresaw that he would be on a steady diet of tranquilizers for the next few days.

He opened the arrival bin and pulled out a handful of paper. One thick bundle was the dossier on Lassen; Walton initialed it and tossed it unread into the Files chute. He would have to rely on Eglin's judgement; Lassen seemed competent enough.

Underneath that, he found the script of the FitzMaugham memorial program to be shown that evening. Walton sat back and started to skim through it.

It was the usual sort of eulogy. He skipped rapidly past FitzMaugham's life and great works, on to the part where Interim Director Walton appeared on the screen to speak.

This part he read more carefully. He was very much interested in the words that Percy had placed in his mouth.

XI

The speech that night went over well ... almost.

Walton watched the program in the privacy of his home, sprawled out on the foamweb sofa with a drink in one hand and the text of Percy's shooting-script in the other. The giant screen that occupied nearly half of his one unbroken wall glowed in lifelike colors.

FitzMaugham's career was traced with pomp and circumstance, done up in full glory: plenty of ringing trumpet flourishes, dozens of eye-appealing color groupings, much high-pitched, tense narrative. Percy had done his job skillfully. The show was punctuated by quotations from FitzMaugham's classic book, *Breathing Space and*

Sanity. Key government figures drifted in and out of the narrative webwork, orating sonorously. That pious fraud, M. Seymour Lanson, President of the United States, delivered a flowery speech; the old figurehead was an artist at his one function, speechmaking. Walton watched, spellbound. Lee Percy was a genius in his field; there was no denying that.

Finally, toward the end of the hour, the narrator said, "The work of Popeek goes on, though its lofty-minded creator lies dead at an assassin's hand. Director FitzMaugham had chosen as his successor a young man schooled in the ideals of Popeek. Roy Walton, we know, will continue the noble task begun by D. F. FitzMaugham."

For the second time that day Walton watched his own face appear on a video screen. He glanced down at the script in his hand and back up at the screen. Percy's technicians had done a brilliant job. The Walton-image on the screen looked so real that the Walton on the couch almost believed he had actually delivered this speech—although he knew it had been cooked up out of some rearranged stills and a few brokendown phonemes with his voice characteristics.

It was a perfectly innocent speech. In humble tones he expressed his veneration for the late director, his hopes that he would be able to fill the void left by the death of FitzMaugham, his sense of Popeek as a sacred trust. Half-listening, Walton began to skim the script.

Startled, Walton looked down at the script. He didn't remember having encountered any such lines on his first reading, and he couldn't find them now. "This morning," the pseudo-Walton on the screen went on, "we received *contact from outer space!* From a faster-than-light ship sent out over a year ago to explore our neighboring stars.

"News of this voyage has been withheld until now for security reasons. But it is my great pleasure to tell you tonight that the stars have at last been reached by man.... A new world waits for us out there, lush, fertile, ready to be colonized by the brave pioneers of tomorrow!"

Walton stared aghast at the screen. His simulacrum had returned now to the script as prepared, but he barely listened.

He was thinking that Percy had let the cat out for sure. It was a totally unauthorized newsbreak. Numbly, Walton watched the program come to its end, and wondered what the repercussions would be once the public grasped all the implications.

He was awakened at 0600 by the chiming of his phone. Grumpily he climbed from bed, snapped on the receiver, switched the cutoff on the picture sender in order to hide his sleep-rumpled appearance, and said, "This is Walton. Yes?"

A picture formed on the screen: a heavily-tanned man in his late forties, stocky, hair close cropped. "Sorry to roust you this way, old man. I'm McLeod."

Walton came fully awake in an instant. "McLeod? Where are you?"

"Out on Long Island. I just pulled into the airport half a moment ago. Traveled all night after dumping the ship at Nairobi."

"You made a good landing, I hope?"

"The best. The ship navigates like a bubble." McLeod frowned worriedly. "They brought me the early-morning telefax while I was having breakfast. I couldn't help reading all about the speech you made last night."

"Oh. I—"

"Quite a crasher of a speech," McLeod went on evenly. "But don't you think it was a little premature of you to release word of my flight. I mean—"

"It was quite premature," Walton said. "A member of my staff inserted that statement into my talk without my knowledge. He'll be disciplined for it."

A puzzled frown appeared on McLeod's face. "But *you* made that speech with your own lips! How can you blame it on a member of your staff?"

"The science that can send a ship to Procyon and back within a year," Walton said, "can also fake a speech. But I imagine we'll be able to cover up the pre-release without too much trouble."

"I'm not so sure of that," said McLeod. He shrugged apologetically. "You see, that planet's there, all right. But it happens to be the property of alien beings who live in the next world. And they're not so happy about having Earth come crashing into their system to colonize!"

Somehow Walton managed to hang onto his self-control, even with this staggering news crashing about him. "You've been in contact with these beings?" he asked.

McLeod nodded. "They have a translating gadget. We met them, yes."

Walton moistened his lips. "I think there's going to be trouble," he said. "I think I may be out of a job, too."

"What's that?"

"Just thinking out loud," Walton said. "Finish your breakfast and meet me at my office at 0900. We'll talk this thing out then."

Walton was in full command of himself by the time he reached the Cullen Building.

He had read the morning telefax and heard the newsblares: they all screamed the sum and essence of Walton's speech of the previous night, and a few of the braver telefax outfits went as far as printing a resumé of the entire speech, boiled down to Basic, of course, for benefit of that substantial segment of the reading public that was most comfortable while moving its lips. The one telefax outfit most outspokenly opposed to Popeek, *Citizen*, took great delight in giving the speech full play, and editorializing on a subsequent sheet against the "veil of security" hazing Popeek operations.

Walton read the *Citizen* editorial twice, savoring its painstaking simplicities of expression. Then he clipped it out neatly and shot it down the chute to public relations, marked *Attention: Lee Percy.*

"There's a Mr. McLeod waiting to see you," his secretary informed him. "He says he has an appointment."

"Send him in," Walton said. "And have Mr. Percy come up here also."

While he waited for McLeod to arrive, Walton riffled through the rest of the telefax sheets. Some of them praised Popeek for having uncovered a new world; others damned them for having hidden news of the faster-than-light drive so long. Walton stacked them neatly in a heap at the edge of his desk.

In the bleak, dark hours of the morning, he had expected to be compelled to resign. Now, he realized, he could immeasurably strengthen his own position if he could control the flow of events and channel them properly.

The square figure of McLeod appeared on the screen. Walton admitted him.

"Sir. I'm McLeod."

"Of course. Won't you sit down?"

McLeod was tense, stiffly formal, very British in his reserve and general bearing. Walton gestured uneasily, trying to cut through the crackle of nervousness.

"We seem to have a mess on our hands," he said. "But there's no mess so messy we can't muddle through it, eh?"

"If we have to, sir. But I can't help feeling this could all have been avoided."

"No. You're wrong, McLeod. If it *could* have been avoided, it would have been avoided. The fact that some idiot in my public relations department gained access to my wire and found out you were returning is incontrovertible; it happened, despite precautions."

"Mr. Percy to see you," the annunciator said.

The angular figure of Lee Percy appeared on the screen. Walton told him to come in.

Percy looked frightened—terrified, Walton thought. He held a folded slip of paper loosely in one hand.

"Good morning, sir."

"Good morning, Lee." Walton observed that the friendly *Roy* had changed to the formal salutation, *sir.* "Did you get the clipping I sent you?"

"Yes, sir." Glumly.

"Lee, this is Leslie McLeod, chief of operations of our successful faster-than-light project. Colonel McLeod, I want you to meet Lee Percy. He's the man who masterminded our little newsbreak last night."

Percy flinched visibly. He stepped forward and laid his slip of paper on Walton's desk. "I m-made a m-mistake last night," he stammered. "I should never have released that break."

"Damned right you shouldn't have," Walton agreed, carefully keeping any hint of severity from his voice. "You have us in considerable hot water, Lee. That planet isn't ours for colonization, despite the enthusiasm with which I allegedly announced it last night. And you ought to be clever enough to realize it's impossible to withdraw and deny good news once you've broken it."

"The planet's not ours? But—?"

"According to Colonel McLeod," Walton said, "the planet is the property of intelligent alien beings who live on a neighboring world, and who no more care to have their system overrun by a pack of Earthmen than we would to have extrasolar aliens settle on Mars."

"Sir, that sheet of paper ..." Percy said in a choked voice. "It's—it's—"

Walton unfolded it. It was Percy's resignation. He read the note carefully twice, smiled, and laid it down. Now was his time to be magnanimous.

"Denied," he said. "We need you on our team, Lee. I'm authorizing a ten percent pay-cut for one week, effective yesterday, but there'll be no other penalty."

"Thank you, sir."

He's crawling to me, Walton thought in amazement. He said, "Only don't pull that stunt again, or I'll not only fire you but blacklist you so hard you won't be able to find work between here and Procyon. Understand?"

"Yes, sir."

"Okay. Go back to your office and get to work. And no more publicity on this faster-than-light thing until I authorize it. No— cancel that. Get out a quick release, a followup on last night. A smoke screen, I mean. Cook up so much cloudy verbiage about the conquest of space that no one bothers to remember anything of what I said. And play down the colonization angle!"

"I get it, sir." Percy grinned feebly.

"I doubt that," Walton snapped. "When you have the release prepared, shoot it up here for my okay. And heaven help you if you deviate from the text I see by as much as a single comma!"

Percy practically backed out of the office.

"Why did you do that?" McLeod asked, puzzled.

"You mean, why did I let him off so lightly?"

McLeod nodded. "In the military," he said, "we'd have a man shot for doing a thing like that."

"This isn't the military," Walton said. "And even though the man behaved like a congenital idiot yesterday, that's not enough evidence to push him into Happysleep. Besides, he knows his stuff. I can't afford to discharge him."

"Are public relations men that hard to come by?"

"No. But he's a good one—and the prospect of having him desert to the other side frightens me. He'll be forever grateful to me now. If I had fired him, he would've had half a dozen anti-Popeek articles in the *Citizen* before the week was out. And they'd ruin us."

McLeod smiled appreciatively. "You handle your job well, Mr. Walton."

"I have to," Walton said. "The director of Popeek is paid to produce two or three miracles per hour. One gets used to it, after a while. Tell me about these aliens, Colonel McLeod."

McLeod swung a briefcase to Walton's desk and flipped the magneseal. He handed Walton a thick sheaf of glossy color photos.

"The first dozen or so are scenes of the planet," McLeod explained. "It's Procyon VIII—number eight out of sixteen, unless we missed a couple. We checked sixteen worlds in the system, anyway. Ten of 'em were methane giants; we didn't even bother to land. Two were ammonia supergiants, even less pleasant. Three small ones had no atmosphere at all worth speaking about, and were no more livable looking than Mercury. And the remaining one was the one we call New Earth. Take a look, sir."

Walton looked. The photos showed rolling hills covered with close-packed shrubbery, flowing rivers, a lovely sunrise. Several of the shots were of indigenous life—a wizened little four-handed monkey, a six-legged doglike thing, a toothy bird.

"Life runs to six limbs there," Walton observed. "But how livable can this place be? Unless your photos are sour, that grass is *blue* ... and the water's peculiar looking, too. What sort of tests did you run?"

"It's the light, sir. Procyon's a double star; that faint companion gets up in the sky and does tricky things to the camera. That grass may look blue, but it's a chlorophyll-based photosynthesizer all the same. And the water's nothing but H_2O, even with that purple tinge."

Walton nodded. "How about the atmosphere?"

"We were breathing it for a week, and no trouble. It's pretty rich in oxygen—twenty-four percent. Gives you a bouncy feeling—just right for pioneers, I'd say."

"You've prepared a full report on this place, haven't you?"

"Of course. It's right here." McLeod started to reach for his briefcase.

"Not just yet," Walton said. "I want to go through the rest of these snapshots." He turned over one after another rapidly until he came to a photo that showed a strange blocky figure, four-armed, bright green in color. Its neckless head was encased in a sort of breathing mask fashioned from some transparent plastic. Three cold, brooding eyes peered outward.

"What's this?" Walton asked.

"Oh, that." McLeod attempted a cheerful grin. "That's a Dirnan.

They live on Procyon IX, one of the ammonia-giant planets. They're the aliens who don't want us there."

XII

Walton stared at the photograph of the alien. There was intelligence there ... yes, intelligence and understanding, and perhaps even a sort of compassion.

He sighed. There were always qualifications, never unalloyed successes.

"Colonel McLeod, how long would it take your ship to return to the Procyon system?" he asked thoughtfully.

McLeod considered the question. "Hardly any time, sir. A few days, maybe. Why?"

"Just a wild idea. Tell me about your contact with these—ah—Dirnans."

"Well, sir, they landed after we'd spent more than a week surveying New Earth. There were six of them, and they had their translating widget with them. They told us who they were, and wanted to know who we were. We told them. They said they ran the Procyon system, and weren't of a mind to let any alien beings come barging in."

"Did they sound hostile?" Walton asked.

"Oh, no. Just businesslike. We were trespassing, and they asked us to get off. They were cold about it, but not angry."

"Fine," Walton said. "Look here, now. Do you think you could go back to their world as—well as an ambassador from Earth? Bring one of the Dirnans here for treaty talks, and such?"

"I suppose so," McLeod said hesitantly. "If it's necessary."

"It looks as if it may be. You had no luck in any of the other nearby systems?"

"No."

"Then Procyon VIII's our main hope. Tell your men we'll offer double pay for this cruise. And make it as fast as you know how."

"Hyperspace travel's practically instantaneous," McLeod said. "We spent most of our time cruising on standard ion drive from planet to planet. Maneuvering in the subspace manifold's a snap, though."

"Good. Snap it up, then. Back to Nairobi and clear out of there as soon as you're ready. Remember, it's urgent you bring one of the aliens here for treaty talks."

"I'll do my best," McLeod said.

Walton stared at the empty seat where McLeod had been, and tried to picture a green Dirnan sitting there, goggling at him with its three eyes.

He was beginning to feel like a juggler. Popeek activity proceeded on so many fronts at once that it quite dazzled him. And every hour there were new challenges to meet, new decisions to make.

At the moment, there were too many eggs and not enough baskets. Walton realized he was making the same mistake FitzMaugham had, that of carrying too much of the Popeek workings inside his skull. If anything happened to him, the operation would be fatally paralyzed, and it would be some time before the gears were meshing again.

He resolved to keep a journal, to record each day a full and mercilessly honest account of each of the many maneuvers in which he was engaged. He would begin with his private conflict with Fred and the interests Fred represented, follow through with the Lamarre-immortality episode, and include a detailed report on the problems of the subsidiary projects, New Earth and Lang's terraforming group.

That gave him another idea. Reaching for his voicewrite, he dictated a concise confidential memorandum instructing Assistant Administrator Eglin to outfit an investigatory mission immediately; purpose, to go to Venus and make contact with Lang. The terraforming group was nearly two weeks overdue in its scheduled report. He could not ignore them any longer.

The everlasting annunciator chimed, and Walton switched on the screen. It was Sellors, and from the look of abject terror on the man's face, Walton knew that something sticky had just transpired.

"What is it, Sellors? Any luck in tracing Lamarre?"

"None, sir," the security chief said. "But there's been another development, Mr. Walton. A most serious one. *Most* serious."

Walton was ready to expect anything—a bulletin announcing the end of the universe, perhaps. "Well, tell me about it," he snapped impatiently.

Sellors seemed about ready to collapse with shame. He said hesitantly, "One of the communications technicians was making a routine check of the building's circuits, Mr. Walton. He found one trunk-line that didn't seem to belong where it was, so he checked up and found out that it had been newly installed."

"Well, what of it?"

"It was a spy pickup with its outlet in your office, sir," Sellors said, letting the words tumble out in one blur. "All the time you were talking this morning, someone was spying on you."

Walton grabbed the arms of his chair. "Are you telling me that your department was blind enough to let someone pipe a spy pickup right into this office?" he demanded. "Where did this outlet go? And is it cut off?"

"They cut it off as soon as they found it, sir. It went to a men's lavatory on the twenty-sixth floor."

"And how long was it in operation?"

"At least since last night, sir. Communications assures me that it couldn't possibly have been there before yesterday afternoon, since they ran a general check then and didn't see it."

Walton groaned. It was small comfort to know that he had had privacy up till last evening; if the wrong people had listened in on his conversation with McLeod, there would be serious trouble.

"All right, Sellors. This thing can't be your fault, but keep your eyes peeled in the future. And tell communications that my office is to be checked for such things twice a day from now on, at 0900 and at 1300."

"Yes, sir." Sellors looked tremendously relieved.

"And start interrogating the communications technicians. Find out who's responsible for that spy circuit, and hold him on security charges. And locate Lamarre!"

"I'll do my best, Mr. Walton."

While the screen was clearing, Walton jotted down a memorandum to himself: *investigate Sellors*. So far, as security chief, Sellors had allowed an assassin to reach FitzMaugham, allowed Prior to burst into Walton's old office, permitted Fred to masquerade as a doorsmith long enough to gain access to Walton's private files, and stood by blindly while Lee Percy tapped into Walton's private wire and some unidentified technician strung a spy pickup into the director's supposedly sacred office.

No security chief could have been as incompetent as all that. It had to be a planned campaign, directed from the outside.

He dialed Eglin.

"Olaf, you get my message about the Venus rescue mission okay?"

"Came through a few minutes ago. I'll have the specs drawn up by tonight."

"Devil with that," Walton said. "Drop everything and send that ship out *now*. I've got to know what Lang and his crew are up to, and I have to know right away. If we don't produce a livable Venus, or at least the possibility of one, in a couple of days, we'll be in for it on all sides."

"Why? What's up?"

"You'll see. Keep an eye on the telefax. I'll bet the next edition of *Citizen* is going to be interesting."

It was.

The glossy sheets of the 1200 *Citizen* extruded themselves from a million receivers in the New York area, but none of those million copies was as avidly pounced on as was Director Walton's. He had been hovering near the wall outlet for ten minutes, avidly awaiting the sheet's arrival.

And he was not disappointed.

The streamer headline ran:

THINGS FROM SPACE NIX BIG POPEEK PLAN

And under it in smaller type:

Greenskinned Uglies Put Feet In Director Walton's Big Mouth

He smiled grimly and went on to the story itself. Written in the best approved *Citizen* journalese, it read:

Fellow human beings, we've been suckered again. The Citizen *found out for sure this morning that the big surprise Popeek's Interim Director Walton yanked out of his hat last night has a hole in it.*

It's sure dope that there's a good planet up there in the sky for grabs. The way we hear it, it's just like earth only prettier, with trees and flowers (remember them?). Our man says the air there is nice and clean. This world sounds okay.

But what Walton didn't know last night came home to roost today. Seems the folks on the next planet out there don't want any sloppy old Earthmen messing up their pasture—and so we ain't going to have any New Earth after all. Wishwashy Walton is a cinch to throw in the towel now.

More dope in later editions. And check the edit page for extra info.

It was obvious, Walton thought, that the spy pickup which had been planted in his office had been a direct pipe line to the *Citizen* news desk. They had taken his conversation with McLeod and carefully ground it down into the chatty, informal, colloquial style that made *Citizen* the world's most heavily-subscribed telefax service.

He shuddered at what might have happened if they'd had their spy pickup installed a day earlier, and overheard Walton in the process of suppressing Lamarre's immortality serum. There would have been a lynch mob storming the Cullen Building ten minutes after the *Citizen* hit the waves with its exposé.

Not that he was much better off now. He no longer had the advantage of secrecy to cloak his actions, and public officials who were compelled to conduct business in the harsh light of public scrutiny generally didn't hold their offices for long.

He turned the sheet over and searched for the editorial column, merely to confirm his expectations.

It was captioned in bold black:

ARE WE PATSIES FOR GREENSKINS?

And went on to say:

Non-human beings have said "Whoa!" to our plans for opening up a new world in space. These aliens have put thumbs down on colonization of the New Earth discovered by Colonel Leslie McLeod.

Aside from the question of why Popeek kept word of the McLeod expedition from the public so long, there is this to consider—will we take this lying down?

We've got to find space for us to live. New Earth is a good place. The answer to the trouble is easy: we take New Earth. If the greenskins don't like it, bounce 'em!

How about it? What do we do? Mr. Walton, we want to know. What goes?

It was an open exhortation to interstellar warfare. Dispiritedly, Walton let the telefax sheets skitter to the floor, and made no move to pick them up.

War with the Dirnans? If *Citizen* had its way, there would be. The telefax sheet would remorselessly stir the people up until the cry for war was unanimous.

Well, thought Walton callously, *a good war would reduce the population surplus. The idiots!*

He caught the afternoon newsblares. They were full of the *Citizen* break, and one commentator made a point-blank demand that Walton either advocate war with the Dirnans or resign.

Not long afterward, UN delegate Ludwig called.

"Some hot action over here today," he told Walton. "After that *Citizen* thing got out, a few of the Oriental delegates started howling for your scalp on sixteen different counts of bungling. What's going on, Walton?"

"Plenty of spy activity, for one thing. The main problem, though, is the nucleus of incompetent assistants surrounding me. I think I'm going to reduce the local population personally before the day is out. With a blunt instrument, preferably."

"Is there any truth in the *Citizen* story?"

"Hell, yes!" Walton exclaimed. "For once, it's gospel! An enterprising telefax man rigged a private pipe line into my office last night and no one caught it until it was too late. Sure, those aliens are holding out. They don't want us coming in there."

Ludwig chewed at his lip. "You have any plans?"

"Dozens of them. Want some, cheap?" He laughed, a brittle, unamused laugh.

"Seriously, Roy. You ought to go on the air again and smooth this thing over. The people are yelling for war with these Dirnans, and half of us over here at the UN aren't even sure the damned creatures exist. Couldn't you fake it up a little?"

"No," Walton said. "There's been enough faking. I'm going on the air with the truth for a change! Better have all your delegates over there listening in, because their ears are in for an opening."

As soon as he was rid of Ludwig he called Lee Percy.

"That program on the conquest of space is almost ready to go," the public relations man informed him.

"Kill it. Have you seen the noon *Citizen?*"

"No; been too busy on the new program. Anything big?"

Walton chuckled. "Fairly big. The *Citizen* just yanked the rug out from under everything. We'll probably be at war with Procyon IX by sundown. I want you to buy me air space on every medium for the 1900 spot tonight."

"Sure thing. What kind of speech you want us to cook up?"

"None at all," Walton said. "I'm going to speak off the cuff for a change. Just buy the time for me, and squeeze the budget for all it's worth."

XIII

The bright light of the video cameras flooded the room. Percy had done a good job; there was a representative from every network, every telefax, every blare of any sort at all. The media had been corralled. Walton's words would echo round the world.

He was seated behind his desk—seated, because he could shape his words more forcefully that way, and also because he was terribly tired. He smiled into the battery of cameras.

"Good evening," he said. "I'm Roy Walton, speaking to you from the offices of the Bureau of Population Equalization. I've been director of Popeek for a little less than a week, now, and I'd like to make a report—a progress report, so to speak.

"We of Popeek regard ourselves as holding a mandate from you, the people. After all, it was the world-wide referendum last year that enabled the United Nations to put us into business. And I want to tell you how the work of Popeek is going.

"Our aim is to provide breathing space for human beings. The world is vastly overcrowded, with its seven billion people. Popeek's job is to ease that overcrowdedness, to equalize the population masses of the world so that the empty portions of the globe are filled up and the extremely overcrowded places thinned out a little. But this is only part of our job—the short-range, temporary part. We're planning for the future here. We know we can't keep shifting population from place to place on Earth; it won't work forever. Eventually every square inch is going to be covered, and then where do we go?

"You know the answer. We go *out*. We reach for the stars. At present we have spaceships that can take us to the planets, but the planets aren't suitable for human life. All right, we'll *make* them suitable! At this very moment a team of engineers is on Venus, in that hot, dry, formaldehyde atmosphere, struggling to turn Venus into a world fit for oxygen-breathing human beings. They'll do it, too—and when they're done with Venus they'll move on to Mars, to the Moon, perhaps to the big satellites of Jupiter and Saturn too. There'll be a day when the solar system will be habitable from Mercury to Pluto— we hope."

"But even that is short-range," Walton said pointedly. "There'll be a day—it may be a hundred years from now, or a thousand, or ten thousand—when the entire solar system will be as crowded with humanity as Earth is today. We have to plan for that day, too. It's the *lack* of planning on the part of our ancestors that's made things so hard for us. We of Popeek don't want to repeat the tragic mistakes of the past.

"My predecessor, the late Director FitzMaugham, was aware of this problem. He succeeded in gathering a group of scientists and technicians who developed a super space drive, a faster-than-light ship that can travel to the stars virtually instantaneously, instead of taking years to make the trip as our present ships would.

"The ship was built and sent out on an exploratory mission. Director FitzMaugham chose to keep this fact a secret. He was afraid of arousing false hopes in case the expedition should be a failure.

"The expedition was *not* a failure! Colonel Leslie McLeod and his men discovered a planet similar to Earth in the system of the star Procyon. I have seen photographs of New Earth, as they have named it, and I can tell you that it is a lovely planet ... and one that will be receptive to our pioneers."

Walton paused a moment before launching into the main subject of his talk.

"Unfortunately, there is a race of intelligent beings living on a neighboring planet of this world. Perhaps you have seen the misleading and inaccurate reports blared today to the effect that these people refuse to allow Earth to colonize in their system. Some of you have cried out for immediate war against these people, the Dirnans.

"I must confirm part of the story the telefax carried today: the Dirnans are definitely not anxious to have Earth set up a colony on a world adjoining theirs. We are strangers to them, and their reaction is understandable. After all, suppose a race of strange-looking creatures landed on Mars, and proceeded with wholesale colonization of our neighboring world? We'd be uneasy, to say the least.

"And so the Dirnans are uneasy. However, I've summoned a Dirnan ambassador—our first diplomatic contact with intelligent alien creatures!—and I hope he'll be on Earth shortly. I plan to convince him that we're peaceful, neighborly people, and that it will be to our mutual benefit to allow Earth colonization in the Procyon system.

"I'm going to need your help. If, while our alien guest is here, he discovers that some misguided Earthmen are demanding war with Dirna, he's certainly not going to think of us as particularly desirable neighbors to welcome with open arms. I want to stress the importance of this. Sure, we can go to war with Dirna for possession of Procyon VIII. But why spread wholesale destruction on two worlds when we can probably achieve our goal peacefully?

"That's all I have to say tonight, people of the world. I hope you'll think about what I've told you. Popeek works twenty-four hours a day in your behalf, but we need your full cooperation if we're going to achieve our aims and bring humanity to its full maturity. Thank you."

———————————————

The floodlights winked out suddenly, leaving Walton momentarily blinded. When he opened his eyes again he saw the cameramen moving their bulky apparatus out of the office quickly and efficiently. The regular programs had returned to the channels—the vapid dancing and joke-making, the terror shows, the kaleidowhirls.

Now that it was over, now that the tension was broken, Walton experienced a moment of bitter disillusionment. He had had high hopes for his speech, but had he really put it over? He wasn't sure.

He glanced up. Lee Percy stood over him.

"Roy, can I say something?" Percy said diffidently.

"Go ahead," Walton said.

"I don't know how many millions I forked over to put you on the media tonight, but I know one thing—we threw a hell of a lot of money away."

Walton sighed wearily. "Why do you say that?"

"That speech of yours," Percy said, "was the speech of an amateur. You ought to let pros handle the big spiels, Roy."

"I thought you liked the impromptu thing I did when they mobbed that Herschelite. How come no go tonight?"

Percy shook his head. "The speech you made outside the building was different. It had emotion; it had punch! But tonight you didn't come across at all."

"No?"

"I'd put money behind it." Acidly Percy said, "You can't win the public opinion by being reasonable. You gave a nice smooth speech. Bland ... folksy. You laid everything on the line where they could see it."

"And that's wrong, is it?" Walton closed his eyes for a moment. "*Why?*"

"Because they won't listen! You gave them a sermon when you should have been punching at them! Sweet reason! You can't be *sweet* if you want to sell your product to seven billion morons!"

"Is that all they are?" Walton asked. "Just morons?"

Percy chuckled. "In the long run, yes. Give them their daily bread and their one room to live in, and they won't give a damn what happens to the world. FitzMaugham sold them Popeek the way you'd sell a car without turbines. He hoodwinked them into buying something they hadn't thought about or wanted."

"They *needed* Popeek, whether they wanted it or not. No one needs a car without turbines."

"Bad analogy, then," Percy said. "But it's true. They don't care a blast about Popeek, except where it affects them. If you'd told them that these aliens would kill them all if they didn't act nice, you'd have gotten across. But this sweetness and light business—oh, no, Roy. It just doesn't work."

"Is that all you have to tell me?" Walton asked.

"I guess so. I just wanted to show you where you had a big chance and muffed it. Where we could have helped you out if you'd let us. I don't want you to think I'm being rude or critical, Roy; I'm just trying to be helpful."

"Okay, Lee. Get out."

"Huh?"

"Go away. Go sell ice to the Eskimos. Leave me alone, yes?"

"If that's the way you want it. Hell, Roy, don't brood over it. We can still fix things up before that alien gets here. We can put the content of tonight's speech across so smoothly that they won't even know we're—"

"*Get out!*"

Percy skittered for the door. He paused and said, "You're all wrought up, Roy. You ought to take a pill or something for your nerves."

Well, he had his answer. An expert evaluation of the content and effect of his speech.

Dammit, he had *tried* to reach them. Percy said he hadn't, and Percy probably was right, little as Walton cared to admit the fact to himself.

But was Percy's approach the only one? Did you have to lie to them, push them, treat them as seven billion morons?

Maybe. Right now billions of human beings—the same human beings Walton was expending so much energy to save—were staring at the kaleidowhirl programs on their videos. Their eyes were getting fixed, glassy. Their mouths were beginning to sag open, their cheeks to wobble, their lips to droop pendulously, as the hypnosis of the color patterns took effect.

This was humanity. They were busy forgetting all the things they had just been forced to listen to. All the big words, like *mandate* and *eventually* and *wholesale destruction*. Just so many harsh syllables to be wiped away by the soothing swirl of the colors.

And somewhere else, possibly, a poet named Prior was listening to his baby's coughing and trying to write a poem—a poem that Walton and a few others would read excitedly, while the billions would ignore it.

Walton saw that Percy was dead right: Roy Walton could never have sold Popeek to the world. But FitzMaugham, that cagy, devious genius, did it. By waving his hands before the public and saying abracadabra, he bamboozled them into approving Popeek before they knew what they were being sold.

It was a lousy trick, but FitzMaugham had realized that it had to be done. Someone had killed him for it, but it was too late by then.

And Walton saw that he had taken the wrong track by trying to be reasonable. Percy's callous description of humanity as "seven billion morons" was uncomfortably close to the truth. Walton would have to make his appeal to a more subliminal level.

Perhaps, he thought, at the level of the kaleidowhirls, those endless patterns of colored light that were the main form of diversion for the Great Unwashed.

I'll get to them, Walton promised himself. *There can't be any dignity or nobility in human life with everyone crammed into one sardine can. So I'll treat them like the sardines they are, and hope I can turn them into the human beings they could be if they only had room.*

He rose, turned out the light, prepared to leave. He wondered if the late Director FitzMaugham had ever faced an internal crisis of this sort, or whether FitzMaugham had known these truths innately from the start.

Probably, the latter was the case. FitzMaugham had been a genius, a sort of superman. But FitzMaugham was dead, and the man who carried on his work was no genius. He was only a mere man.

The reports started filtering in the next morning. It went much as Percy had predicted.

Citizen was the most virulent. Under the sprawling headline, *WHO'S KIDDING WHO?* the telefax sheet wanted to know what the "mealy-mouthed" Popeek director was trying to tell the world on all media the night before. They weren't sure, since Walton, according to *Citizen*, had been talking in "hifalutin prose picked on purpose to befuddle John Q. Public." But their general impression was that Walton had proposed some sort of sellout to the Dirnans.

The sellout idea prevailed in most of the cheap telefax sheets.

"Behind a cloud of words, Popeek czar Walton is selling the world downstream to the greenskins," said one paper. "His talk last night was strictly bunk. His holy-holy words and grim face were supposed to put over something, but we ain't fooled—and don't you be fooled either, friend!"

The video commentators were a little kinder, but not very. One called for a full investigation of the Earth-Dirna situation. Another wanted to know why Walton, an appointed official and not even a permanent one at that, had taken it upon himself to handle such high-power negotiations. The UN seemed a little worried about that, even though Ludwig had made a passionate speech insisting that negotiations with Dirna were part of Walton's allotted responsibilities.

That touched off a new ruckus. "How much power does Walton have?" *Citizen* demanded in a later edition. "Is he the boss of the world? And if he is, who the devil is he anyway?"

That struck Walton harder than all the other blows. He had been gradually realizing that he did, in fact, control what amounted to dictatorial powers over the world. But he had not yet fully admitted it to himself, and it hurt to be accused of it publicly.

One thing was clear: his attempt at sincerity and clarity had been a total failure. The world was accustomed to subterfuge and verbal pyrotechnics, and when it didn't get the expected commodity, it grew suspicious. Sincerity had no market value. By going before the public and making a direct appeal, Walton had aroused the suspicion that he had something hidden up his sleeve.

When *Citizen's* third edition of the day openly screamed for war with Dirna, Walton realized the time had come to stop playing it clean. From now on, he would chart his course and head there at any cost.

He tore a sheet of paper from his memo pad and inscribed on it a brief motto: *The ends justify the means!*

With that as his guide, he was ready to get down to work.

XIV

Martinez, security head for the entire Appalachia district, was a small, slight man with unruly hair and deep, piercing eyes. He stared levelly at Walton and said, "Sellors has been with security for twenty years. It's absurd to suggest that he's disloyal."

"He's made a great many mistakes," Walton remarked. "I'm simply suggesting that if he's not utterly incompetent he must be in someone else's pay."

"And you want us to break a man on your say-so, Director Walton?" Martinez shook his head fussily. "I'm afraid I can't see that. Of course, if you're willing to go through the usual channels, you could conceivably request a change of personnel in this district. But I don't see how else—"

"Sellors will have to go," Walton said. "Our operation has sprung too many leaks. We'll need a new man in here at once, and I want you to double-check him personally."

Martinez rose. The little man's nostrils flickered ominously. "I refuse. Security is external to whims and fancies. If I remove Sellors, it will undermine security self-confidence all throughout the country."

"All right," sighed Walton. "Sellors stays. I'll file a request to have him transferred, though."

"I'll pigeonhole it. I can vouch for Sellors' competence myself," Martinez snapped. "Popeek is in good hands, Mr. Walton. Please believe that."

Martinez left. Walton glowered at the retreating figure. He knew Martinez was honest—but the security head was a stubborn man, and rather than admit the existence of a flaw in the security structure he had erected, Martinez would let a weak man continue in a vital position.

Well, that blind spot in Martinez' makeup would have to be compensated for, Walton thought. One way or another, he would have to get rid of Sellors and replace him with a security man he could trust.

He scribbled a hasty note and sent it down the chute to Lee Percy. As Walton anticipated, the public relations man phoned minutes later.

"Roy, what's this release you want me to get out? It's fantastic—Sellors a spy? How? He hasn't even been arrested. I just saw him in the building."

Walton smirked. "Since when do you have such a high respect for accuracy?" he asked. "Send out the release and we'll watch what happens."

The 1140 newsblares were the first to carry the news. Walton listened cheerlessly as they revealed that Security Chief Sellors had been arrested on charges of disloyalty. According to informed sources, said the blares, Sellors was now in custody and had agreed to reveal the nature of the secret conspiracy which had hired him.

At 1210 came a later report: Security Chief Sellors had temporarily been released from custody.

And at 1230 came a still later report: Security Chief Sellors had been assassinated by an unknown hand outside the Cullen Building.

Walton listened to the reports with cold detachment. He had foreseen the move: Sellors' panicky employers had silenced the man for good. *The ends justify the means*, Walton told himself. There was no reason to feel pity for Sellors; he had been a spy and death was the penalty. It made no real difference whether death came in a federal gas chamber or as the result of some carefully faked news releases.

Martinez called almost immediately after word of Sellors' murder reached the blares. The little man's face was deadly pale.

"I owe you an apology," he said. "I acted like an idiot this morning."

"Don't blame yourself," Walton said. "It was only natural that you'd trust Sellors; you'd known him so long. But you can't trust anyone these days, Martinez. Not even yourself."

"I will have to resign," the security man said.

"No. It wasn't your fault. Sellors was a spy and a bungler, and he paid the price. His own men struck him down when that rumor escaped that he was going to inform. Just send me a new man, as I asked—and make him a good one!"

Keeler, the new security attaché, was a crisp-looking man in his early thirties. He reported directly to Walton as soon as he reached the building.

"You're Sellors' replacement, eh? Glad to see you, Keeler." Walton studied him. He looked tough and hard and thoroughly incorruptible. "I've a couple of jobs I'd like you to start on right away. First, you know Sellors was looking for a man named Lamarre. Let me fill you in on that, and—"

"No need for that," Keeler said. "I was the man Sellors put on the Lamarre chase. There isn't a trace of him anywhere. We've got feelers out all over the planet now, and no luck."

"Hmm." Walton was mildly annoyed; he had been wishfully hoping Sellors had found Lamarre and had simply covered up the fact. But if Keeler had been the one who handled the search, there was no hope of that.

"All right," Walton said. "Keep on the hunt for Lamarre. At the moment I want you to give this building a thorough scouring. There's no telling how many spy pickups Sellors planted here. Top to bottom, and report back to me when the job is done."

Next on Walton's schedule was a call from communications. He received it and a technician told him, "There's been a call from the Venus ship. Do you want it, sir?"

"Of course!"

"It says, 'Arrived Venus June fifteen late, no sign of Lang outfit yet. Well keep looking and will report daily.' It's signed, 'Spencer.'"

"Okay," Walton said. "Thanks. And if any further word from them comes, let me have it right away."

The fate of the Lang expedition, Walton reflected, was not of immediate importance. But he would like to know what had happened to the group. He hoped Spencer and his rescue mission had something more concrete to report tomorrow.

The annunciator chimed. "Dr. Frederic Walton is on the line, sir. He says it's urgent."

"Okay," Walton said. He switched over and waited for his brother's face to appear on the screen. A nervous current of anticipation throbbed in him.

"Well, Fred?" he asked at length.

"You've been a busy little bee, haven't you?" Fred said. "I

understand you have a new security chief to watch over you."

"I don't have time to make conversation now," Walton snapped.

"Nor do I. You fooled us badly, with that newsbreak on Sellors. You forced us into wiping out a useful contact prematurely."

"Not so useful," Walton said. "I was on to him. If you hadn't killed him, I would have had to handle the job myself. You saved me the trouble."

"My, my! Getting ruthless, aren't we!"

"When the occasion demands," Walton said.

"Fair enough. We'll play the same way." Fred's eyes narrowed. "You recall our conversation in the Bronze Room the other day, Roy?"

"Vividly."

"I've called to ask for your decision," Fred said. "One way or the other."

Walton was caught off guard. "But you said I had a week's grace!"

"The period has been halved," Fred said. "We now see it's necessary to accelerate things."

"Tell me what you want me to do. Then I'll give you my answer."

"It's simple enough. You're to resign in my favor. If it's not done by nightfall tomorrow, we'll find it necessary to release the Lamarre serum. Those are our terms, and don't try to bargain with me."

Walton was silent for a moment, contemplating his brother's cold face on the screen. Finally he said, "It takes time to get such things done. I can't just resign overnight."

"FitzMaugham did."

"Ah, yes—if you call that a resignation. But unless you want to inherit the same sort of chaos I did, you'd better give me a little time to prepare things."

Fred's eyes gleamed. "Does that mean you'll yield? You'll resign in my favor?"

"There's no guarantee the UN will accept you," Walton warned. "Even with my recommendation, I can't promise a one hundred percent chance of success."

"We'll have to risk it," said Fred. "The important step is getting you out of there. When can I have confirmation of all this?"

Walton eyed his brother shrewdly. "Come up to my office tomorrow at this time. I'll have everything set up for you by then, and I'll be able to show you how the Popeek machinery works. That's one advantage you'll have over me. FitzMaugham kept half the workings in his head."

Fred grinned savagely. "I'll see you then, Roy." Chuckling, he added, "I knew all that ruthlessness of yours was just skin deep. You never were tough, Roy."

Walton glanced at his watch after Fred had left the screen. The time was 1100. It had been a busy morning.

But some of the vaguenesses were beginning to look sharper. He knew, for instance, that Sellors had been in the pay of the same organization that backed Fred. Presumably, this meant that FitzMaugham had been assassinated by the landed gentry.

But for what reason? Surely, not simply for the sake of assassination. Had they cared to, they might have killed FitzMaugham whenever they pleased.

He saw now why the assassination had been timed as it had. By the time the conspirators had realized that Walton was sure to be the old man's successor, Fred had already joined their group. They had ready leverage on the prospective director. They knew they could shove him out of office almost as quickly as he got in, and supplant him with their puppet, Fred.

Well, they were in for a surprise. Fred was due to appear at Walton's office at 1100 on the morning of the seventeenth to take over command. Walton planned to be ready for them by then.

There was the matter of Lamarre. Walton wanted the little scientist and his formula badly. But by this time Fred had certainly made at least one copy of Lamarre's documents; the threat would remain, whether or not Popeek recovered the originals.

Walton had twenty-four hours to act. He called up Sue Llewellyn, Popeek's comptroller.

"Sue, how's our budget looking?"

"What's on your mind, Roy?"

"Plenty. I want to know if I can make an expenditure of—say, a billion, between now and nightfall."

"A *billion*? You joking, Roy?"

"Hardly." Walton's tone was grim. "I hope I won't need it all. But there's a big purchase I want to make ... an investment. Can you squeeze out the money? It doesn't matter where you squeeze it from, either, because if we don't get it by nightfall there probably won't be a Popeek by the day after tomorrow."

"What *are* you talking about, Roy?"

"Give me a yes or no answer. And if the answer's not the one I want to hear, I'm afraid you can start looking for a new job, Sue."

She uttered a little gasp. Then she said, "Okay, Roy. I'll play along with you, even if it bankrupts us. There's a billion at your disposal as of now, though Lord knows what I'll use for a payroll next week."

"You'll have it back," Walton promised. "With compound interest."

His next call was to a man he had once dealt with in his capacity of secretary to Senator FitzMaugham. He was Noel Hervey, a registered securities and exchange slyster.

Hervey was a small, worried-looking little man, but his unflickering eyes belied his ratty appearance. "What troubles you, Roy?"

"I want you to make a stock purchase for me, pronto. Within an hour, say?"

Hervey shook his head instantly. "Sorry, Roy. I'm all tied up on a hefty monorail deal. Won't be free until Wednesday or Thursday, if by then."

Walton said, "What sort of money will you be making on this big deal of yours, Noel?"

"Confidential! You wouldn't invade a man's privacy on a delicate matter like—"

"Will it be worth five million dollars for you, Noel?"

"Five million—hey, is this a gag?"

"I'm awfully serious," Walton said. "I want you to swing a deal for me, right away. You've heard my price."

Hervey smiled warmly. "Well, start talking, friend. Consider me hired."

———

A few other matters remained to be tended to hurriedly. Walton spent some moments talking to a communications technician, then sent out an order for three or four technical books—*Basic Kaleidowhirl Theory* and related works. He sent a note to Lee Percy requesting him to stop by and see him in an hour, and told his annunciator that for no reason whatsoever was he to be disturbed for the next sixty minutes.

The hour passed rapidly; by its end, Walton's head was slightly dizzy from too much skimming, but his mind was thrumming with new possibilities, with communications potentials galore. Talk about reaching people! He had a natural!

He flipped on the annunciator. "Is Mr. Percy here yet?"

"No, sir. Should I send for him?"

"Yes. He's due here any minute to see me. Have there been any calls?"

"Quite a few. I've relayed them down to Mr. Eglin's office, as instructed."

"Good girl," Walton said.

"Oh, Mr. Percy's here. And there's a call for you from communications."

Walton frowned. "Tell Percy to wait outside a minute or two. Give me the call."

The communications tech on the screen was grinning excitedly. He said, "Subspace message just came in for you, sir."

"From Venus?"

"No, sir. From Colonel McLeod."

"Let's have it," Walton said.

The technician read, "'To Walton from McLeod, via subspace radio: Have made successful voyage to Procyon system, and am on way back with Dirnan ambassador on board. See you soon, and good luck—you'll need it.'"

"Good. That all?"

"That's all, sir."

"Okay. Keep me posted." He broke contact and turned to the annunciator. Excitement put a faint quiver in his voice. "You can send in Mr. Percy now," he said.

XV

Walton looked up at the public relations man and said, "How much do you know about kaleidowhirls, Lee?"

"Not a hell of a lot. I never watch the things, myself. They're bad for the eyes."

Walton smiled. "That makes you a nonconformist, doesn't it? According to the figures I have here, the nightly kaleidowhirl programs are top-ranked on the rating charts."

"Maybe so," Percy said cautiously. "I still don't like to watch them. What goes, Roy?"

"I've suddenly become very interested in kaleidowhirls myself," Walton said. He leaned back and added casually, "I think they can be used as propaganda devices. My brother's reaction to one gave me the idea, couple days ago, at the Bronze Room. For the past hour or so, I've been studying kaleidowhirls in terms of information theory. Did you know that it's possible to get messages across via kaleidowhirl?"

"Of course," Percy gasped. "But the Communications Commission would never let you get away with it!"

"By the time the Communications Commission found out what had been done," Walton said calmly, "we wouldn't be doing it any more. They won't be able to prove a thing." Sarcastically he added, "After spending a lifetime in public relations, you're not suddenly getting a rush of ethics, are you?"

"Well ... let's have the details, then."

"Simple enough," Walton said. "We feed through a verbal message—something like *Hooray for Popeek* or *I Don't Want War With Dirna*. We flash it on the screen for, say, a microsecond, then cover it up with kaleidowhirl patterns. Wait two minutes, then flash it again. Plenty of noise, but the signal will get through if we flash it often enough."

"And it'll get through deep down," Percy said. "Subliminally. They won't even realize that they're being indoctrinated, but suddenly they'll have a new set of opinions about Popeek and Dirna!" He shuddered. "Roy, I hate to think what can happen if someone else gets to thinking about this and puts on his own kaleidowhirl show."

"I've thought of that. After the Dirna crisis is over—after we've put over our point—I'm going to take steps to make sure no one can use this sort of weapon again. I'm going to frame someone into putting on a propaganda kaleidowhirl, and then catch him in the act. That ought to be sufficient to wise up the Communications

Commission."

"In other words," Percy said, "you're willing to use this technique *now*. But since you don't want anyone else to use it, you're willing to give up future use of it yourself as soon as the Dirna trouble is over."

"Exactly." Walton shoved the stack of textbooks over to the PR man. "Read these through first. Get yourself familiar with the setup. Then buy a kaleidowhirl hour and get a bunch of our engineers in there to handle the special inserts. Okay?"

"It's nasty, but I like it. When do you want the program to begin?"

"Tomorrow. Tonight, if you can work it. And set up a poll of some kind to keep check on the program's effectiveness. I want two messages kaleidowhirled alternately: one supporting Popeek, one demanding a peaceful settlement with the aliens. Have your pulse takers feel out the populace on those two propositions, and report any fluctuation to me immediately."

"Got it."

"Oh, one more thing. I suspect you'll have some extra responsibilities as of tomorrow, Lee."

"Eh?"

"Your office will have one additional medium to deal with. Telefax. I'm buying *Citizen* and we're going to turn it into a pro-Popeek rag."

Percy's mouth dropped in astonishment; then he started to laugh. "You're a wonder, Roy. A genuine wonder."

———

Moments after Percy departed, Noel Hervey, the security and exchange slyster, called.

"Well?" Walton asked.

Hervey looked preoccupied. "I've successfully spent a couple of hundred million of Popeek's money in the last half-hour, Roy. You now own the single biggest block of *Citizen* stock there is."

"How much is that?"

"One hundred fifty-two thousand shares. Approximately thirty-three percent."

"Thirty-three percent! What about the other eighteen percent?"

"Patience, lad, patience. I know my job. I snapped up all the small holdings there were, very quietly. It cost me a pretty penny to farm out the purchases, too."

"Why'd you do that?" Walton asked.

"Because this has to be handled very gingerly. You know the ownership setup of *Citizen*?"

"No."

"Well, it goes like this: Amalgamated Telefax owns a twenty-six percent chunk, and Horace Murlin owns twenty-five percent. Since Murlin also owns Amalgamated, he votes fifty-one percent of the stock, even though it isn't registered that way. The other forty-nine percent doesn't matter, Murlin figures. So I'm busy gathering up as much of it as I can for you—under half a dozen different brokerage names. I doubt that I can get it all, but I figure on rounding up at least forty-nine percent. Then I'll approach Murlin with a Big Deal and sucker him into selling me six percent of his *Citizen* stock. He'll check around, find out that the remaining stock is splintered ninety-seven different ways, and he'll probably let go of a little of his, figuring he still has control."

"Suppose he doesn't?" Walton asked.

"Don't worry," Hervey said confidently. "He will. I've got a billion smackers to play with, don't I? I'll cook up a deal so juicy he can't resist it—and all he'll have to do to take a flyer will be to peel off a little of his *Citizen* stock. The second he does that, I transfer all the fragmented stock to you. With your controlling majority of fifty-one percent, you boot Murlin off the Board, and the telefax sheet is yours! Simple? Clear?"

"Perfectly," Walton said. "Okay. Keep in touch."

He broke contact and walked to the window. The street was packed with people scrambling in every direction, like so many ants moving at random over the ground. Many of them clutched telefax sheets—and the most popular one was the *Citizen*. Many of them would gape and goggle at kaleidowhirl programs, come evening.

Walton suddenly tightened his fist. In just that way, he thought, Popeek was tightening its hold on the public by capturing the mass media. If Hervey's confidence had any justification in truth, they would own the leading anti-Popeek telefax sheet by tomorrow. With subtle handling over the course of several days, they could swing the slant of *Citizen* around to a pro-Popeek stand, and do it so surreptitiously that it would seem as though the sheet had never had any other policy.

As for the kaleidowhirl subterfuge—that, Walton admitted, was hitting below the belt. But he had resolved that all would be fair during the current crisis. There would be time enough for morality after war had been averted.

At about 1430 that day, Walton took advantage of a lull in activities to have a late lunch at the Bronze Room. He felt that he had to get away from the confining walls of his office for at least some part of the afternoon.

The Bronze Room had adopted cerise as its color scheme for the day. Walton selected a private room, lunched lightly on baked chlorella steak and filtered rum, and dialed a twelve-minute nap. When the alarm system in the foamweb couch stirred him to wakefulness, he stretched happily, some of the choking tension having been washed out of him.

Thoughtfully, he switched on the electroluminescent kaleidoscope and stared at it. It worked on the same principle as the kaleidowhirl programs beamed over the public video, except that the Bronze Room provided closed-channel beaming of its own kaleidoscopic patterns; tending more to soft greens and pale rose, they were on a higher esthetic plane, certainly, than the jagged, melodramatic purples and reds the video channels sent out for popular consumption.

But it was with a certain new apprehension that Walton now studied the kaleidoscopic pattern. Now that he knew what a dangerous weapon the flashing colors could be, how could he be certain that the Bronze Room proprietors were not flashing some scarcely seen subliminal command at him this very moment?

He turned the set off with a brusque gesture.

The ends justify the means. A nice homily, he thought, which allowed him to do almost anything. It brought to mind the rationale of Ivan Karamazov: without God, everything is permissible.

But both God and Dostoevski seem to be obsolete these days, he reminded himself. God is now a lean young man with an office on the twenty-ninth floor of the Cullen Building—and as for Dostoevski, all he did was write books, and therefore could not have been of any great importance.

He felt a tremor of self-doubt. Maybe it had been unwise to let kaleidowhirl propaganda loose on the world; once unleashed, it might not be so easily caged again. He realized that as soon as the Popeek campaign was over, he would have to make sure some method was devised for pre-checking all public and closed-channel kaleidoscopic patterns.

The most damnable part of such propaganda techniques, he knew, was that you could put over almost any idea at all without arousing suspicion on the part of the viewer. He wouldn't know he'd been tampered with; you could tell him so, after the new idea had been planted, and by then he wouldn't believe you.

Walton dialed another filtered rum, and lifted it to his lips with a slightly shaky hand.

"Mr. Ludwig of the United Nations called while you were out, sir," Walton was told upon returning to his office. "He'd like you to call him back."

"Very well. Make the connection for me."

When Ludwig appeared, Walton said, "Sorry I missed your call. What's happening?"

"Special session of the Security Council just broke up. They passed a resolution unanimously and shipped it on to the Assembly. There's going to be an immediate hearing to determine the new permanent head of Popeek."

Walton clamped his lips together. After a moment he said, "How come?"

"The Dirnan crisis. They don't want a mere interim director handling things. They feel the man dealing with the aliens ought to have full UN blessing."

"Should I interpret that to mean I get the job automatically?"

"I couldn't swear to it," said Ludwig. "General consensus certainly favors you to continue. I'd advise that you show up at the hearing in person and present your program in detail; otherwise they may stick some smooth-talking politico in your place. The noise is slated to start at 1100, day after tomorrow. The eighteenth."

"I'll be there," Walton said. "Thanks for the tip."

He chewed the end of his stylus for a moment, then hastily scribbled down the appointment. As of now, he knew he couldn't worry too strongly about events taking place the day after tomorrow—not with Fred arriving for a show-down the next morning.

The next day began busily enough. Hervey was the first to call.

"The *Citizen's* sewed up, Roy! I had dinner with Murlin last night and weaseled him out of four percent of *Citizen*stock in exchange for a fancy tip on the new monorail project out Nevada way. He was grinning all over the place—but I'll bet he's grinning out of the other side of his mouth this morning."

"Is it all arranged?" Walton asked.

"In the bag. I was up by 0700 and consolidating my holdings—*your* holdings, I mean. Forty-seven percent of the stock I had fragmented in a dozen different outfits; the other two percent outstanding belonged to rich widows who wouldn't sell. I lumped the forty-seven percent together in your name, then completed the transfer on Murlin's four percent and stuck that in there too. *Citizen* telefax is now the property of Popeek, Roy!"

"Fine work. How much did it cost?"

Then he said, "Four hundred eighty-three million and some change. Plus my usual five percent commission, which in this case comes to about two and a quarter million."

"But I offered you five million," Walton said. "That offer still goes."

"You want me to lose my license? I spend years placing bribes to get a slyster's license, and you want me to throw it away for an extra couple million? Uh-uh. I'll settle for two and a quarter, and damn good doing I call that for a day's work."

Walton grinned. "You win. And Sue Llewellyn will be glad to know it didn't cost the whole billion to grab *Citizen*. You'll be over with the papers, won't you?"

"About 1000," the slyster said. "I've gotta follow through for Murlin on his monorail deal first. The poor sucker! See you in an hour."

"Right."

Rapidly Walton scribbled memos. As soon as the papers were in his hands, he'd serve notice on Murlin that a stock-holders' meeting was to be held at once. After that, he'd depose Murlin, fire the present *Citizen* editors, and pack the telefax sheet with men loyal to

Popeek.

Fred was due at 1100. Walton buzzed Keeler, the new security chief, and said, "Keeler, I have an appointment with someone at 1100. I want you to station three men outside my door and frisk him for weapons as he comes in."

"We'd do that anyway, sir. It's standard procedure now."

"Good. But I want you to be one of the three. And make sure the two who come with you are tight-mouthed. I don't want *any* newsbreaks on this."

"Right, sir."

"Okay. Be there about 1050 or so. About 1115, I'm going to press my door opener, and I want you and your men to break in, arrest my visitor, and spirit him off to the deepest dungeon security has. And leave him there. If Martinez wants to know what's going on, tell him I'll take responsibility."

Keeler looked vaguely puzzled, but merely nodded. "We frisk him first, then let him talk to you for fifteen minutes. Then we come in on signal and take him away. I've got it."

"This man's a dangerous anti-Popeek conspirator. Make sure he's drugged before he gets out of my office. I don't want him making noise."

The annunciator sounded. "Man from communications has a message for you, Mr. Walton."

He switched over from Keeler to communications and said, "Go ahead."

"From McLeod, Mr. Walton. We just got it. It says, 'Arriving Nairobi on the 18th, will be in your office with Dirnan following morning if he feels like making the trip. Otherwise will you come to Nairobi?'"

"Tell him yes, if necessary," Walton said.

He glanced at his watch. 0917. It looked like it was going to be hectic all day.

And Fred was due at 1100.

XVI

Hervey showed up at 1003, grinning broadly. He unfolded a thick wad of documents and thrust them at Walton.

"I hold in my hand the world's most potent telefax sheet," Hervey said. He flipped the documents casually onto Walton's desk and laughed. "They're all yours. Fifty-one percent, every bit of it voting stock. I told Murlin about it just before I left him this morning. He turned purple."

"What did he say?"

"What *could* he say? I asked him offhandedly if he knew where all the outstanding *Citizen* stock was, and he said yes, it was being held by a lot of small holders. And then I told him that somebody was buying out the small holders, and that I was selling my four percent to him. That's when he started to change colors. When I left he was busy making phone calls, but I don't think he'll like what he's going to find out."

Walton riffled through the papers. "It's all here, eh? Fine work. I'll put through your voucher in half an hour or so, unless you're in a hurry."

"Oh, don't rush," Hervey said. He ran a finger inside his collar. "Couple of security boys outside, y'know. They really gave me a going-over."

"I'm expecting an assassin at 1100," Walton said lightly. "They're on the lookout."

"Oh? A close friend?"

"A relative," Walton said.

Fred arrived promptly at 1100. By that time Walton had already set the machinery in operation for the taking-over of *Citizen*.

The first step had been to call Horace Murlin and confirm the fact that Popeek now owned the telefax sheet. Murlin's fleshy face was a curious shade of rose-purple; he sputtered at Walton for five minutes before admitting he was beaten.

With Murlin out of the way, Walton selected a new editorial staff for the paper from a list Percy supplied. He intended to keep the reporting crew of the old regime intact; *Citizen* had a fantastically efficient newsgathering team, and there was no point in breaking it up. It was the policy-making level Walton was interested in controlling.

The 1000 edition of *Citizen* was the last under the old editors. They had received word from Murlin about what had happened, and by 1030, when Walton sent his dismissal notices over, they were already cleaning out their desks.

That 1000 edition was a beauty, though. The lead headline read:

ARE WE CHUMPS FOR THE GREENSKINS?

And most of the issue was devoted to inflammatory pro-war anti-Popeek journalism. A full page of "letters from the readers"—actually transcribed phone calls, since few of *Citizen's* readers were interested in writing letters—echoed the editorial stand. One "letter" in particular caught Walton's attention.

It was from a Mrs. P.F. of New York City Environ, which probably meant Jersey or lower Connecticut, and it was short and to the point:

To the Editor—

Horray for you. Popeek is a damned crime and that Walton criminal ought to be put away and we ought to kill those greenskins up there before they kill us. We gotta have room to live.

Kill them before they kill us. Walton snickered. All the old hysterias, the old panic reactions, come boiling up again in times of stress.

He looked at his hand. It was perfectly steady, even though his wrist watch told him Fred would be here in just a few minutes. A week ago, a situation like this would have had him gobbling benzolurethrin as fast as he could unwrap the lozenges.

The ghostly presence of FitzMaugham seemed to hover in the room. *The ends justify the means*, Walton told himself grimly, as he waited for his brother to arrive.

Fred was dressed completely in black, from his stylish neo-Victorian waistcoat and the bit of ribbon at his throat to the mirror-bright leather pumps on his feet. The splendor of his clothing was curiously at odds with the coarseness of his features and the stockiness of his body.

He walked into Walton's office at the stroke of 1100 and sighed deeply—the sigh of a man about to take permanent possession. "Good morning, Roy. I'm on time, as always."

"And looking radiant, my dear brother." Walton gestured appreciatively at Fred's clothes. "It's been a long time since I've seen you in anything but your lab smock."

"I gave notice at the lab yesterday night after I spoke to you. I'm no longer an employee of Popeek. And I felt I should dress with the dignity suitable to my new rank." He grinned buoyantly. "Well, ready to turn over the orb and scepter, Roy?"

"Not exactly," Walton said.

"But—"

"But I promised you I'd resign in your favor today, Fred. I don't think I ever used those words, but I certainly implied it, didn't I?"

"Of course you did. You told me to come here at 1100 and you'd arrange the transfer."

Walton nodded. "Exactly so." He waited a long moment and then said quietly, "I lied, Fred."

He had chosen the words carefully, for maximum impact. He had not chosen wrongly.

For a brief instant Fred's face was very pale against the blackness of his garb. Total disbelief flickered across his eyes and mouth.

Walton had considered his brother's mental picture of him—the elder brother, virtuous, devoted to hard work, kind to animals, and just a little soft in the head. Also, extremely honest.

Fred hadn't expected Walton to be lying. And the calm admission stunned him.

"You're not planning to go through with it, then?" Fred asked in a dead voice.

"No."

"You realize what this means in terms of the serum, don't you? The moment I get out of here and transmit your refusal to my employers, they'll begin wholesale manufacture and distribution of the Lamarre serum. The publicity won't be good, Roy. Nor the result."

"You won't get out of here," Walton said.

Another shock wave rippled over Fred's face. "You can't be serious, Roy. My employers know where I am; they know what I'm here for. If they don't hear from me within twenty-four hours, they'll proceed with serum distribution. You can't hope to—"

"I'll risk it," Walton interrupted. "If nothing else, I'll have a twenty-four extension. You didn't really think I could hand Popeek over to you on a platter, Fred? Why, I don't even know how secure my *own* position is here. So I'm afraid I'll have to back down on my offer. You're under arrest, Fred!"

"*Arrest!*" Fred sprang from his seat and circled around the desk toward Walton. For a moment the two brothers stared at each other, faces inches apart. Walton put one hand on his brother's shoulder and, gripping tightly, forced him around to the front of the desk.

"You had this all planned, didn't you?" Fred said bitterly. "Yesterday, when you talked to me, you knew this was what you were going to do. But you said you'd yield, and I believed you! I don't fool easy, but I thought I had you pegged because you were my brother. I *knew* you. You wouldn't do a sneaky thing like this."

"But I did," Walton said.

Suddenly, Fred jumped. He charged at Walton blindly, head down.

In the same motion, Walton signaled for Keeler and his men to break in, and met Fred's charge. He caught his brother in midstride with a swinging punch that sent his head cracking back sharply.

Fred's face twisted and writhed, more in astonishment than pain. He stepped back, rubbing his chin. "You've changed," he said. "This job's made you tough. A year ago you would never have done this to me."

Walton shrugged. "Look behind you, Fred. And this time you can trust me."

Fred turned warily. Keeler and two other gray-clad security men stood there.

"Drug him and take him away," Walton said. "Have him held in custody until I notify Martinez."

Fred's eyes widened. "You're a *dictator!*" he said hoarsely. "You just move people around like chessmen, Roy. Like chessmen."

"Drug him," Walton repeated.

Keeler stepped forward, a tiny hypodermic spray cupped in his hand. He activated it with a twitch of his thumb and touched it to Fred's forearm. A momentary hum droned in the office as the vibrating spray forced the drug into Fred's arm.

He slumped like an empty sack. "Pick him up," Keeler ordered. "Take him and let's get going."

The story broke in the 1300 edition of *Citizen*, and from the general tone of the piece Walton could see the fine hand of Lee Percy at work.

The headline was:

GUY TRIES TO KNOCK OFF POPEEK HEAD

After the usual string of subheads, all in the cheerful, breezy, barely literate *Citizen* style, came the body of the story:

A guy tried to bump Popeek top number Roy Walton today. Security men got there in time to keep Walton from getting the same finisher as dead Popeek boss FitzMaugham got last week.

Walton says he's all right; the assassin didn't even come close. He also told our man that he expects good news on the New Earth bit soon. We like the sound of those words. Popeek may be with the stream after all. Who knows?

The voice was that of *Citizen*, but the man behind the voice was thinking a little differently. Had the previous editors of *Citizen* been handling the break, the prevailing tone would most likely have been too-bad-he-missed.

Walton called Percy after the edition came out. "Nice job you did on our first *Citizen*," he said approvingly. "It's just what I want: same illiterate style, but a slow swerving of editorial slant until it's completely pro-Popeek."

"Wait till you see tomorrow's paper. We're just getting the hang of it! And we'll have our first kaleidowhirl show at 2000 tonight. Cost a fortune to buy in, but we figured that's the best hour."

"What's the buried message?"

"As you said," Percy told him. "A pro-Popeek job and some pacifist stuff. We've got a team of pollsters out now, and they say the current's predominantly going the other way. We'll be able to tell if the kaleidowhirl stuff works out, all right."

"Keep up the good work," Walton said. "We'll get there yet. The alien isn't due to arrive for another day or so—McLeod gets into Nairobi tomorrow some time. I'm going to testify before the UN tomorrow, too. I hope those UN boys are watching our pretty color patterns tonight."

Percy grinned. "Boy, you bet!"

Walton threw himself energetically into his work. It was taking shape, now. There were still some loose ends, of course, but he was beginning to feel that some end to the tangle of interlocking intrigues was in sight.

He checked with a public recreation director and discovered there would be a block forum on West 382nd Street at 1830 that night. He made a note to attend, and arranged to have a synthetic mask fashioned so he wouldn't have to reveal his own identity.

Twenty-four hours. In that time, Fred's employers would presumably be readying themselves to loose Lamarre's serum on the world; an extraterrestrial being would be landing on Earth—and, by then, Walton would have been called to render an account of his stewardship before the United Nations.

The annunciator chimed again. "Yes?" Walton said.

"Mr. O'Mealia of Mount Palomar Observatory, calling long distance to talk to you, sir."

"Put him on," Walton said puzzledly.

O'Mealia was a red-faced individual with deep-set, compelling eyes. He introduced himself as a member of the research staff at Mount Palomar. "Glad I could finally reach you," he said, in a staccato burst of words. "Been trying to call for an hour. Made some early-morning observations of Venus a little while ago, and I thought you'd be interested."

"Venus? What?"

"Cloud blanket looks awfully funny, Mr. Walton. Blazing away like sixty. Got the whole staff down here to discuss it, and the way it looks to us there's some sort of atomic chain-reaction going on in Venus' atmosphere. I think it's those terraforming men you Popeek folk have up there. I think they've blown the whole place up!"

XVII

Walton stepped off the jetbus at Broadway and West 382nd Street, paused for a moment beneath a street lamp, and fingered his chin to see if his mask were on properly. It was.

Three youths stood leaning against a nearby building. "Could you tell me where the block meeting's being held?" Walton asked.

"Down the street and turn left. You a telefax man?"

"Just an interested citizen," Walton said. "Thanks for the directions."

It was easy to see where the block meeting was; Walton saw streams of determined-looking men and women entering a bulky old building just off 382nd Street. He joined them and found himself carried along into the auditorium.

Nervously he found a seat. The auditorium was an old one, predominantly dark brown and cavernous, with row after row of hard wooden folding chairs. Someone was adjusting a microphone on stage. A sharp metallic whine came over the public-address system.

"Testing. Testing, one two three...."

"It's all right, Max!" someone yelled from the rear. Walton didn't turn around to look.

A low undercurrent of murmuring was audible. It was only 1815; the meeting was not due to start for another fifteen minutes, but the hall was nearly full, with more than a thousand of the local residents already on hand.

The fifteen minutes passed slowly. Walton listened carefully to the conversations around him; no one was discussing the Venus situation. Apparently his cloud of censorship had been effective. He had instructed Percy to keep all word of the disaster from the public until the 2100 newsblares. By that time, the people would have been exposed to the indoctrinating kaleidowhirl program at 2000, and their reaction would be accordingly more temperate—he hoped.

Also, releasing the news early would have further complicated the survey Walton was trying to make by attending this public meeting. The Index of Public Confusion increased factorially; one extra consideration for discussion and Walton's task would be hopelessly difficult.

At exactly 1830, a tall, middle-aged man stepped out on the stage. He seized the microphone as if it were a twig and said, "Hello, folks. Glad to see you're all here tonight. This is an important meeting for us all. In case some of you don't know me—and I do see some new faces out there—I'm Dave Forman, president of the West 382nd Street Association. I also run a little law business on the side, just to help pay the rent." (Giggles.)

"As usual in these meetings," Forman went on, "we'll have a brief panel discussion, and then I'll throw the thing open to you folks for floor discussion. The panelists tonight are people you all know— Sadie Hargreave, Dominic Campobello, Rudi Steinfeld. Come on out here, folks."

The panelists appeared on the stage diffidently. Sadie Hargreave was a short, stout, fierce-looking little woman; Campobello was chunky, balding, Steinfeld tall and ascetic. Walton was astonished that there should be such camaraderie here. Was it all synthetic? It didn't seem that way.

He had always remained aloof, never mingling with his neighbors in the gigantic project where he lived, never suspecting the existence of community life on this scale. But, somehow, community life had sprung up in this most Gargantuan of cities. Organizations within each project, within each block perhaps, had arisen, converting New York into an interlocking series of small towns. *I ought to investigate the grass roots more often*, Walton thought. *Caliph Haroun-al-Raschid having a night on the town.*

"Hello, folks," Sadie Hargreave said aggressively. "I'm glad I can talk to you tonight. Gosh, I want to speak out. I think it's crazy to let these thing-men from outer space push us around. I for one feel we ought to take strong action against that space world."

Cries of "Yeah! Yeah! Go to it, Sadie!" rose from the audience.

Skillfully she presented three inflammatory arguments in favor of war with Dirna, backing up each with a referent of high emotional connotation. Walton watched her performance with growing admiration. The woman was a born public relations technician. It was too bad she was on the other side of the fence.

He saw the effect she had: people were nodding in agreement, grimacing vehemently, muttering to themselves. The mood of the meeting, he gathered, was overwhelmingly in favor of war if Dirna did not yield New Earth.

Dominic Campobello began his address by inviting all and sundry to his barber shop; this was greeted with laughter. Then he launched into a discourse on Popeek as an enemy of mankind. A few catcalls, Walton noted, but again chiefly approval. Campobello seemed sincere.

The third man, Rudi Steinfeld, was a local music teacher. He, too, spoke out against Popeek, though in a restrained, dryly intellectual manner. People began yawning. Steinfeld cut his speech short.

It was now 1900. In one hour Percy's kaleidowhirl program would be screened.

Walton stayed at the block meeting until 1930, listening to citizen after citizen rise and heap curses upon Popeek, Dirna, or Walton, depending on where his particular ire lay. At 1930 Walton rose and left the hall.

He phoned Percy. "I'm on West 382nd Street. Just attended a block meeting. I'd say the prevailing sentiment runs about ninety percent agin us. We don't have the people backing our program any more, Lee."

"We never did. But I think we'll nail 'em now. The kaleidowhirl's ready to go, and it's a honey. And I think *Citizen*will sell 'em too! We're on our way, Roy."

"I hope so," Walton said.

He was unable to bring himself to watch Percy's program, even though he reached his room in time that night. He knew there could be no harm in watching—at least not for him—but the idea of voluntarily submitting his mind to external tampering was too repugnant to accept.

Instead he spent the hour dictating a report on the block meeting, for benefit of his pollster staff. When he was done with that, he turned to the 2100 edition of *Citizen*, which came clicking from the telefax slot right on schedule.

He had to look hard for the Venus story. Finally he found it tucked away at the bottom of the sheet.

ACCIDENT ON VENUS

A big blowup took place on the planet Venus earlier today. Sky-men who watched the popoff say it was caused by an atomic explosion in the planet's atmosphere.

Meanwhile, attempts are being made to reach the team of Earth engineers working on Venus. No word from them yet. They may be dead.

Walton chuckled. *They may be dead,* indeed! By now Lang and his team, and the rescue mission as well, lay dead under showers of radioactive formaldehyde, and Venus had been turned into a blazing hell ten times less livable than it had been before.

Percy had mishandled the news superbly. For one thing, he had carefully neglected to link Lang with Popeek in any way. That was good connotative thinking. It would be senseless to identify Popeek in the public mind with disasters or fiascos of any kind.

For another, the skimpy insignificance of the piece implied that it had been some natural phenomenon that sent Venus up in flames, not the fumbling attempts of the terraformers. Good handling there, too.

Walton felt cheerful. He slept soundly, knowing that the public consciousness was being properly shaped.

By 0900, when he arrived at his office, the pollsters had reported a ten percent swing in public opinion, in the direction of Popeek and Walton. At 1000, *Citizen* hit the slots with an extra announcing that prospects for peaceful occupation of New Earth looked excellent. The editorial praised Walton. The letters-to-the-editor column, carefully fabricated by Lee Percy, showed a definite upswing of opinion.

The trend continued, and it was contagious. By 1100, when Walton left the Cullen Building and caught a jetcopter for United Nations Headquarters, the pro-Popeek trend in public opinion was almost overwhelming.

The copter put down before the gleaming green-glass facade of UN Headquarters; Walton handed the man a bill and went inside, where a tense-faced Ludwig was waiting for him.

"They started early," Ludwig said. "It's been going on since 1000."

"How do things look?"

"I'm puzzled, Roy. Couple of die-hards are screaming for your scalp, but you're getting help from unexpected quarters. Old Mogens Snorreson of Denmark suddenly got up and said it was necessary for the safety of mankind that we give you a permanent appointment as director of Popeek."

"*Snorreson?* But hasn't he been the one who wanted me bounced?"

Ludwig nodded. "That's what I mean. The climate is changing, definitely changing. Ride the crest, Roy. The way things look now, you may end up being swept into office for life."

They entered the giant Assembly hall. At the dais, a black-faced man with bright teeth was speaking.

"Who's that?" Walton whispered.

"Malcolm Nbono, the delegate from Ghana. He regards you as a sort of saint for our times."

Walton slipped into a seat in the gallery and said, "Let's listen from here before we go down below. I want to catch my breath."

The young man from Ghana was saying, "... Crisis points are common to humanity. Many years ago, when my people came from their colonial status and achieved independence, we learned that painstaking negotiations and peaceful approaches are infinitely more efficacious than frontal attack by violent means. In my eyes, Roy Walton is an outstanding exponent of this philosophy. I urge his election as director of the Bureau of Population Equalization."

A heavy-bearded, ponderous man to Nbono's right shouted "Bravo!" at that point, and added several thick Scandinavian expletives.

"That's good old Mogens. The Dane really is on your side this morning," Ludwig said.

"Must have been watching the kaleidowhirl last night," Walton murmured.

The delegate from Ghana concluded with a brief tremolo cadenza praising Walton. Walton's eyes were a little moist; he hadn't realized he was a saint. Nbono tacked on an abrupt coda and sat down.

"All right," Walton said. "Let's go down there."

They made a grand entrance. Ludwig took his seat behind the neon *United States* sign, and Walton slid into the unoccupied seat to Ludwig's right. A definite stir of interest was noticeable.

The secretary-general was presiding—beady-eyed Lars Magnusson of Sweden. "I see Mr. Walton of Popeek has arrived," he commented. "By a resolution passed unanimously yesterday, we have invited Mr. Walton this morning to address us briefly. Mr. Walton, would you care to speak now?"

"Thank you very much," Walton said. He rose.

The delegates were staring at him with great interest ... and, somewhere behind them, obscured by the bright lights of the cameras, there were, he sensed, a vast multitude of onlookers peering at him from the galleries.

Onlookers who had seen Percy's kaleidowhirl last night, evidently. A thunderous wave of applause swept down on him. *This is too easy,* he thought. *That kaleidowhirl program seems to have hypnotized everybody.*

He moistened his lips.

"Mr. Secretary-General, members of the Assembly, friends: I'm very grateful for this chance to come before you on my own behalf. It's my understanding that you are to choose a permanent successor to Mr. FitzMaugham today. I offer myself as a candidate for that post."

He had planned a long, impassioned, semantically loaded speech to sway them, but the happenings thus far this morning convinced him it was unnecessary. The kaleidowhirl had done the work for him.

"My qualifications for the post should be apparent to all. I worked with the late Director FitzMaugham during the formative days of Popeek. Upon his death I succeeded to his post and have efficiently maintained the operation of the Bureau during the eight days since his assassination.

"There are special circumstances which dictate my continuation in office. Perhaps you know of the failure of our terraforming experiments—the destruction of our outpost on Venus, and the permanent damage done to that planet. The failure of this project makes it imperative that we move outward to the stars to relieve our population crisis."

He took a deep breath. "In exactly four hours," he said, "a representative of an alien race will land on Earth to confer with the director of Popeek. I cannot stress too greatly the importance of maintaining a continuity of thought and action within our Bureau. Bluntly, it is essential that *I* be the one who deals with this alien. I ask for your support. Thank you."

He took his seat again. Ludwig was staring at him, aghast.

"Roy! What kind of a speech was that? You can't just *demand* the job! You've got to give reasons! You have to—"

"Hush," Walton said. "Don't worry about it. Were you watching the kaleidowhirls last night?"

"Me? Of course not!"

Walton grinned. "*They* were," he said, gesturing at the other delegates. "I'm not worried."

XVIII

Walton left the Assembly meeting about 1215, pleading urgent Popeek business. The voting began at 1300, and half an hour later the result was officially released.

The 1400 *Citizen* was the first to carry the report.

WALTON ELECTED POPEEK HEAD

The General Assembly of the United Nations gave Roy Walton a healthy vote of confidence today. By a 95-0 vote, three abstaining, he was picked to succeed the late D. F. FitzMaugham as Popeek czar. He has held the post on a temporary basis for the past eight days.

Walton rang up Percy. "Who wrote that *Citizen* piece on me?" he asked.

"I did, chief. Why?"

"Nicely done, but not enough sock. Get all those three-syllable words out of it by the next edition. Get back to the old *Citizen* style of jazzy writing."

"We thought we'd brush it up a little now that you're in," Percy said.

"No. That's dangerous. Keep to the old style, but revamp the content. We're rolling along, now. What's new from the pollsters?"

"Fifty percent swing to Popeek. You're the most popular man in the country, as of noon. Churches are offering up prayers for you. There's a move afoot to make you President of the United States in place of old Lanson."

"Let Lanson keep his job," Walton chuckled. "I'm not looking for any figurehead jobs. I'm too young. When's the next *Citizen* due?"

"At 1500. We're keeping up hourly editions until the crisis is over."

Walton thought for a moment. "I think 1500's too early. The Dirnan arrives in Nairobi at 1530 our time. I want a big splash in the 1600 edition—but not a word before then!"

"I'm with you," Percy said, and signed off.

A moment later the annunciator said, "There's a closed-circuit call for you from Batavia, sir."

"From where?"

"Batavia. Java."

"Let's have it," Walton said.

A fleshy face filled the screen, the face of a man who had lived a soft life in a moist climate. A rumbling voice said, "You are Walton."

"I am Walton."

"I am Gaetano di Cassio. Pleased of making the acquaintance, Signor Director Walton. I own rubber plantation in the area here."

Walton's mind immediately clocked off the top name on the list of landed proprietors Lassen had prepared for him:

di Cassio, Gaetano. 57. Holdings estimated at better than a billion and a quarter. Born Genoa 2175, settled in Amsterdam 2199. Purchased large Java holding 2211.

"What can I do for you, Mr. di Cassio?"

The rubber magnate looked ill; his fleshy face was beaded with globules of sweat. "Your brother," he grunted heavily. "Your brother worked for me. I sent him to see you yesterday. He has not come back."

"Indeed?" Walton shrugged. "There's a famous phrase I could use at this point. I won't."

"Make no flippancies," di Cassio said heavily. "Where is he?"

Walton said, "In jail. Attempted coercion of a public official." He realized di Cassio was twice as nervous and tense as he was.

"You have jailed him," di Cassio repeated flatly. "Ah, I see. Jail." The audio pickup brought in the sound of stertorous breathing. "Will you not free him?" di Cassio asked.

"I will not."

"Did he not tell you what would happen if he would not be granted his request?"

"He told me," Walton said. "Well?"

The fat man looked sick. Walton saw that the bluff was going to be unsuccessful; that the conspirators would not dare put Lamarre's drug into open production. It had been a weapon without weight, and Walton had not let himself be cowed by it.

"Well?" Walton repeated inflexibly.

"You trouble me sorely," said di Cassio. "You give my heart pain, Mr. Walton. Steps will have to be taken."

"The Lamarre immortality serum—"

The face on the screen turned a leaden gray. "The serum," di Cassio said, "is not entered into this talking."

"Oh, no? My brother Fred made a few remarks—"

"Serum *non esiste!*"

Walton smiled calmly. "A nonexistent serum," he said, "has, unfortunately, nonexistent leverage against me. You don't scare me, di Cassio. I've outbluffed you. Go take a walk around your plantation. While you still have it, that is."

"Steps will be taken," di Cassio said. But his malevolence was hollow. Walton laughed and broke contact.

He drew Lassen's list from his desk and inscribed a brief memo to Olaf Eglin on it. These were the hundred biggest estates in the world. Within a week, there would be equalized Japanese living on all of them.

He called Martinez of security. "I've ordered my brother Fred remanded to your care," he said.

"I know." The security man sounded peeved. "We can't hold a man indefinitely, not even on your say-so, Director Walton."

"The charge is conspiracy," Walton said. "Conspiracy against the successful operation of Popeek. I'll have a list of the ringleaders on your desk in half an hour. I want them rounded up, given a thorough psyching, and jailed."

"There are times," Martinez said slowly, "when I suspect you exceed your powers, Director Walton. But send me the list and I'll have the arrests made."

The afternoon crawled. Walton proceeded with routine work on half a dozen fronts, held screened conferences with each of his section chiefs, read reports augmenting what he already knew of the Venus disaster, and gobbled a few benzolurethrin tranquilizers.

He called Keeler and learned that no sign of Lamarre had come to light yet. From Percy he discovered that *Citizen* had added two hundred thousand subscribers overnight. The 1500 edition had a lengthy editorial praising Walton, and some letters that Percy swore were genuine, doing the same.

At 1515 Olaf Eglin called to announce that the big estates were in the process of being dismembered. "You'll be able to hear the howls from here to Batavia when we get going," Eglin warned.

"We have to be tough," Walton told him firmly.

At 1517 he devoted a few minutes to a scientific paper that proposed terraforming Pluto by establishing synthetic hydrogen-fusion suns on the icy planet. Walton skimmed through the specifications, which involved passing a current of several million amperes through a tube containing a mixture of tritium and deuterium. The general idea, he gathered, was to create electromagnetic forces of near-solar intensity; a pulsed-reaction engine would supply a hundred megawatts of power continuously at 10,000,000 degrees centigrade.

Has possibilities, Walton noted, and forwarded the plan on to Eglin. It sounded plausible enough, but Walton was personally skeptical of undertaking any more terraforming experiments after the Venus fiasco. There were, after all, limits to the public relations miracles Lee Percy could create.

At 1535 the annunciator chimed again. "Call from Nairobi, Africa, Mr. Walton."

"Okay."

McLeod appeared on the screen.

"We're here," he said. "Arrived safely half a microsecond ago, and all's well."

"How about the alien?"

"We have him in a specially constructed cabin. Breathes hydrogen and ammonia, you know. He's very anxious to see you. When can you come?"

Walton thought for a moment. "I guess there's no way of transporting him here, is there?"

"I wouldn't advise it. The Dirnans are very sensitive about traveling in such a low gravitational field. Makes their stomachs queasy, you know. Do you think you could come out here?"

"When's the earliest?"

"Oh—half an hour?" McLeod suggested.

"I'm on my way," said Walton.

The sprawling metropolis of Nairobi, capital of the Republic of Kenya, lay at the foot of the Kikuyu Hills, and magnificent Mount Kilimanjaro towered above it. Four million people inhabited Nairobi, finest of the many fine cities along Africa's western coast. Africa's Negro republics had built soundly and well after achieving their liberation from colonial status.

The city was calm as Walton's special jet decelerated for landing at the vast Nairobi airport. He had left at 1547 New York time; the transatlantic trip had taken two hours and some minutes, and there was an eight-hour time zone differential between Kenya and New York. It was now 0313 in Nairobi; the early-morning rain was falling right on schedule as the jet taxied to a halt.

McLeod was there to meet him. "The ship's in the hills, five miles out of town. There's a copter waiting for you here."

Moments after leaving the jetliner, Walton was shepherded aboard the 'copter. Rotors whirred; the 'copter rose perpendicularly until it hung just above the cloud-seeders at 13,000 feet, then fired its jets and streaked toward the hills.

It was not raining when they landed; according to McLeod, the night rain was scheduled for 0200 in this sector, and the seeders had already been here and moved on to bring rain to the city proper. A groundcar waited for them at the airstrip in the hills. McLeod drove, handling the turboelectric job with skill.

"There's the ship," he said proudly, pointing.

Walton felt a sudden throat lump.

The ship stood on its tail in the midst of a wide, flat swath of jet-blackened concrete. It was at least five hundred feet high, a towering pale needle shimmering brightly in the moonlight. Wideswept tailjets supported it like arching buttresses. Men moved busily about in the floodlighted area at its base.

McLeod drove up to the ship and around it. The flawless symmetry of the foreside was not duplicated behind; there, a spidery catwalk ran some eighty feet up the side of the ship to a gaping lock, and by its side a crude elevator shaft rose to the same hatch.

McLeod drew efficient salutes from the men as he left the car; Walton, only puzzled glares.

"We'd better take the elevator," McLeod said. "The men are working on the catwalk."

Silently they rode up into the ship. They stepped through the open airlock into a paneled lounge, then into narrow companionways. McLeod paused and pressed down a stud in an alcove along the way.

"I'm back," he announced. "Tell Thogran Klayrn that I've brought Walton. Find out whether he'll come out to talk to him."

"I thought he had to breathe special atmosphere," Walton said. "How can he come out?"

"They've got breathing masks. Usually they don't like to use them." McLeod listened at the earpiece for a moment, then nodded. To Walton he said, "The alien will see you in the lounge."

———————————

Walton had barely time to fortify himself with a slug of filtered rum when a crewman appeared at the entrance to the lounge and declared ostentatiously, "His Excellency, Thogran Klayrn of Dirna."

The alien entered.

Walton had seen the photographs, and so he was partially prepared. But only partially.

The photos had not given him any idea of size. The alien stood eight feet high, and gave an appearance of astonishing mass. It must have weighed four or five hundred pounds, but it stood on two thick legs barely three feet long. Somewhere near the middle of the columnar body, four sturdy arms jutted forth strangely. A neckless head topped the ponderous creature—a head covered entirely with the transparent breathing mask. One of the hands held a mechanical device of some sort; the translating machine, Walton surmised.

The alien's hide was bright-green, and leathery in texture. A faint pungent odor drifted through the room, as of an object long immersed in ammonia.

"I am Thogran Klayrn," a booming voice said. "Diplomasiarch of Dirna. I have been sent to talk with Roy Walton. Are you Roy Walton?"

"I am." Walton's voice sounded cold and dry to his own ears. He knew he was too tense, pressing too hard. "I'm very glad to meet you, Thogran Klayrn."

"Please sit. I do not. My body is not made that way."

Walton sat. It made him feel uncomfortable to have to crane his neck upward at the alien, but that could not be helped. "Did you have a pleasant trip?" Walton asked, temporizing desperately.

A half-grunt came from Thogran Klayrn. "Indeed it was so. But I do not indulge in little talk. A problem we have, and it must be discussed."

"Agreed." Whatever a diplomasiarch might be on Dirna, it was *not* a typical diplomat. Walton was relieved that it would not be necessary to spend hours in formalities before they reached the main problem.

"A ship sent out by your people," the alien said, "invaded our system some time ago. In command was your Colonel McLeod, whom I have come to know well. What was the purpose of this ship?"

"To explore the worlds of the universe and to discover a planet where we of Earth could settle. Our world is very overcrowded now."

"So I have been given to know. You have chosen Labura—or, in your terms, Procyon VIII—as your colony. Is this so?"

"Yes," Walton said. "It's a perfect world for our purposes. But Colonel McLeod has informed me that you object to our settling there."

"We do so object." The Dirnan's voice was cold. "You are a young and active race. We do not know what danger you may bring to us. To have you as our neighbors—"

"We could swear a treaty of eternal peace," Walton said.

"Words. Mere words."

"But don't you see that we can't even *land* on that planet of yours! It's too big, too heavy for us. What possible harm could we do?"

"There are races," said the Dirnan heavily, "which believe in violence as a sacred act. You have long-range missiles. How might we trust you?"

Walton squirmed; then sudden inspiration struck him. "There's a planet in this system that's as suitable for your people as Labura is for ours. I mean Jupiter. We could offer you colonial rights to Jupiter in exchange for the privilege of colonizing Labura!"

The alien was silent for a moment. Considering? There was no way of telling what emotions passed across that face. At length the alien said, "Not satisfactory. Our people have long since reached stability of population. We have no need of colonies. It has been many thousands of your years since we have ventured into space."

Walton felt chilled. *Many thousands of years!* He realized he was up against a formidable life form.

"We have learned to stabilize births and deaths," the Dirnan went on sonorously. "It is a fundamental law of the universe, and one that you Earthfolk must learn sooner or later. How you choose to do it is your own business. But we have no need of planets in your system, and we fear allowing you to enter ours. The matter is simple of statement, difficult of resolution. But we are open to suggestions from you."

Walton's mind blanked. Suggestions? What possible suggestion could he make?

He gasped. "We have something to offer," he said. "It might be of value to a race that has achieved population stability. We would give it to you in exchange for colonization rights."

"What is this commodity?" the Dirnan asked.

"Immortality," Walton said.

XIX

He returned to New York alone, later that night, too tired to sleep and too wide awake to relax. He felt like a poker player who had triumphantly topped four kings with four aces, and now was fumbling in his hand trying to locate some of those aces for his skeptical opponents.

The alien had accepted his offer. That was the one solid fact he was able to cling to, on the lonely night ride back from Nairobi. The rest was a quicksand of ifs and maybes.

If Lamarre could be found....

If the serum actually had any value....

If it was equally effective on Earthmen and Dirnans....

Walton tried to dismiss the alternatives. He had made a desperately wild offer, and it had been accepted. New Earth was open for colonization, *if*....

The world outside the jet was a dark blur. He had left Nairobi at 0518 Nairobi time; jetting back across the eight intervening time zones, he would arrive in New York around midnight. Ultrarapid jet transit made such things possible; he would live twice through the early hours of June nineteenth.

New York had a fifteen minute rain scheduled at 0100 that night. Walton reached the housing project where he lived just as the rain was turned on. The night was otherwise a little muggy; he paused outside the main entrance, letting the drops fall on him. After a few minutes, feeling faintly foolish and very tired, he went inside, shook himself dry, and went to bed. He did not sleep.

Four caffeine tablets helped him get off to a running start in the morning. He arrived at the Cullen Building early, about 0835, and spent some time bringing his private journal up to date, explaining in detail the burden of his interview with the alien ambassador. Some day, Walton thought, a historian of the future would discover his journal and find that for a short period in 2232 a man named Roy Walton had acted as absolute dictator of humanity. The odd thing, Walton reflected, was that he had absolutely no power drive: he had been pitchforked into the role, and each of his successive extra-legal steps had been taken quite genuinely in the name of humanity.

Rationalization? Perhaps. But a necessary one.

At 0900 Walton took a deep breath and called Keeler of security. The security man smiled oddly and said, "I was just about to call you, sir. We have some news, at last."

"News? What?"

"Lamarre. We found his body this morning, just about an hour ago. Murdered. It turned up in Marseilles, pretty badly decomposed, but we ran a full check and the retinal's absolutely Lamarre's."

"Oh," Walton said leadenly. His head swam. "Definitely Lamarre," he repeated. "Thanks, Keeler. Fine work. Fine."

"Something wrong, sir? You look—"

"I'm very tired," Walton said. "That's all. Tired. Thanks, Keeler."

"You called me about something, sir," Keeler reminded him gently.

"Oh, I was calling about Lamarre. I guess there's no point in— thanks, Keeler." He broke the contact.

For the first time Walton felt total despair, and, out of despair, came a sort of deathlike calmness. With Lamarre dead, his only hope of obtaining the serum was to free Fred and wangle the notes from him. But Fred's price for the notes would be Walton's job. Full circle, and a dead end.

Perhaps Fred could be induced to reveal the whereabouts of the notes. It wasn't likely, but it was possible. And if not? Walton shrugged. A man could do only so much. Terraforming had proved a failure, equalization was a stopgap of limited value, and the one extrasolar planet worth colonizing was held by aliens. Dead end.

I tried, Walton thought. *Now let someone else try.*

He shook his head, trying to clear the fog of negation that suddenly surrounded him. His thinking was all wrong; he had to keep trying, had to investigate every possible avenue before giving up.

His fingers hovered lightly over a benzolurethrin tablet, then drew back. Stiffly he rose from his chair and switched on the annunciator.

"I'm leaving the office for a while," he said hoarsely. "Send all calls to Mr. Eglin."

He had to see Fred.

Security Keep was a big, blocky building beyond the city limits proper, a windowless tower near Nyack, New York. Walton's private jetcopter dropped noiselessly to the landing stage on the wide parapet of the building. He contemplated its dull-bronze metallic exterior for a moment.

"Should I wait here?" the pilot asked.

"Yes," Walton said. With accession to the permanent directorship he rated a private ship and a live pilot. "I won't be here long."

He left the landing stage and stepped within an indicated screener field. There was a long pause. The air up here, Walton thought, is fresh and clean, not like city air.

A voice said, "What is your business here?"

"I'm Walton, director of Popeek. I have an appointment with Security Head Martinez."

"Wait a moment, Director Walton."

None of the obsequious *sirring* and *pleasing* Walton had grown accustomed to. In its way, the bluntness of address was as refreshing as the unpolluted air.

Walton's keen ears detected a gentle electronic whirr; he was being thoroughly scanned. After a moment the metal door before him rose silently into a hidden slot, and he found himself facing an inner door of burnished copper.

A screen was set in the inner door.

Martinez' face confronted him.

"Good morning, Director Walton. You're here for our interview?"

"Yes."

The inner door closed. This time, two chunky atomic cannons came barreling down to face him snout first. Walton flinched involuntarily, but a smiling Martinez stepped before them and greeted him. "Well, why are you here?"

"To see a prisoner of yours. My brother, Fred."

Martinez frowned and passed a delicate hand through his rumpled hair. "Seeing prisoners is positively forbidden, Mr. Walton. Seeing them in person, that is. I could arrange a closed-circuit video screening for you."

"Forbidden? But the man's here on my word alone. I—"

"Your powers, Mr. Walton, are still somewhat less than infinite. This is one rule we never have relaxed, and never will. The prisoners in the Keep are under constant security surveillance, and your presence in the cell block would undermine our entire system. Will video do?"

"I guess it'll have to," Walton said. He was not of a mind to argue now.

"Come with me, then," said Martinez.

The little man led him down a dim corridor into a side room, one entire wall of which was an unlit video screen. "You'll have total privacy in here," Martinez assured him. He did things to a dial set in the right-hand wall, and murmured a few words. The screen began to glow.

"You can call me when you're through," Martinez said. He seemed to glide out of the room, leaving Walton alone with Fred.

The huge screen was like a window directly into Fred's cell. Walton met his brother's bitter gaze head on.

Fred looked demonic. His eyes were ringed by black shadows; his hair was uncombed, his heavy-featured face unwashed. He said, "Welcome to my palatial abode, dearest brother."

"Fred, don't make it hard for me. I came here to try to clarify things. I didn't *want* to stick you away here. I *had* to."

Fred smiled balefully. "You don't need to apologize. It was entirely my fault. I underestimated you; I didn't realize you had changed. I thought you were the same old soft-hearted dope I grew up with. You aren't."

"Possibly." Walton wished he had taken that benzolurethrin after all. Every nerve in his body seemed to be jumping. He said, "I found out today that Lamarre's dead."

"So?"

"So there's no possible way for Popeek to obtain the immortality serum except through you. Fred, I need that serum. I've promised it to the alien in exchange for colonization rights on Procyon VIII."

"A neat little package deal," Fred said harshly. "*Quid pro quo*. Well, I hate to spoil it, but I'm not going to tell where the *quo* lies hidden. You're not getting that serum out of me."

"I can have you mind blasted," Walton said. "They'll pick your mind apart and strip it away layer by layer until they find what they want. There won't be much of *you* left by then, but we'll have the serum."

"No go. Not even you can swing that deal," Fred said. "You can't get a mind-pick permit on your lonesome: you need the President's okay. It takes at least a day to go through channels—half a day, if you pull rank. And by that time, Roy, I'll be out of here."

"What?"

"You heard me clear enough. *Out*. Seems you're holding me here on pretty tenuous grounds. Habeas corpus hasn't been suspended yet, Roy, and Popeek isn't big enough to do it. I've got a writ. I'll be sprung at 1500 today."

"I'll have you back in by 1530," Walton said angrily. "We're picking up di Cassio and that whole bunch. That'll be sufficient grounds to quash your habeas corpus."

"Ah! Maybe so," Fred said. "But I'll be out of here for half an hour. That's long enough to let the world know how you exercised an illegal special privilege and spared Philip Prior from Happysleep. Wiggle out of that one, then."

Walton began to sweat.

Fred had him neatly nailed this time.

Someone in security evidently had let him sneak his plea out of the Keep. Martinez? Well, it didn't matter. By 1500 Fred would be free, and the long-suppressed Prior incident would be smeared all over the telefax system. That would finish Walton; affairs were at too delicate an impasse for him to risk having to defend himself now. Fred might not be able to save himself, but he could certainly topple his brother.

There was no possible way to get a mind-pick request through before 1500; President Lanson himself would have to sign the authorization, and the old dodderer would take his time about it.

Mind picking was out, but there was still one weapon left to the head of Popeek, if he cared to use it. Walton moistened his lips.

"It sounds very neat," he said. "I'll ask you one more time: will you yield Lamarre's serum to me for use in my negotiations with the Dirnan?"

"Are you kidding? No!" Fred said positively. "Not to save your life or mine. I've got you exactly where I want you, Roy. Where I've wanted you all my life. And you can't wriggle out of it."

"I think you've underestimated me again," Walton said in a quiet voice. "And for the last time."

He stood up and opened the door of the room. A gray-clad security man hovered outside.

"Will you tell Mr. Martinez I'm ready to leave?" Walton said.

The jetcopter pilot was dozing when Walton reached the landing stage. Walton woke him and said, "Let's get back to the Cullen Building, fast."

The trip took about ten minutes. Walton entered his office, signaling his return but indicating he wanted no calls just yet. Carefully, thoughtfully, he arranged the various strands of circumstance in his mind, building them into a symmetrical structure.

Di Cassio and the other conspirators would be rounded up by nightfall, certainly. But no time element operated there; Walton knew he could get mind-pick authorizations in a day or so, and go through one after another of them until the whereabouts of Lamarre's formula turned up. It was brutal, but necessary.

Fred was a different problem. Unless Walton prevented it, he'd be freed on his writ within hours—and when he revealed the Prior incident, it would smash Walton's whole fragile construct to flinders.

He couldn't fight habeas corpus. But the director of Popeek did have one weapon that legally superseded all others. Fred had gambled on his brother's softness, and Fred had lost.

Walton reached for his voicewrite and, in a calm, controlled voice, began to dictate an order for the immediate removal of Frederic Walton from Security Keep, and for his prompt transference to the Euthanasia Clinic on grounds of criminal insanity.

XX

Even after that—for which he felt no guilt, only relief—Walton felt oppressive foreboding hanging over him. Martinez phoned, late that day, to inform him that the hundred landowners had been duly corralled and were being held in the lower reaches of Security Keep.

"They're yelling and squalling," Martinez said, "and they'll have plenty of high-power legal authority down here soon enough. You'd better have a case against them."

"I'm obtaining an authorization to mind blast the one named di Cassio. He's the ringleader, I think." Walton paused for a moment, then asked, "Did a Popeek copter arrive to pick up Frederic Walton?"

"Yes," Martinez said. "At 1406. A lawyer showed up here waving a writ, a little while later, but naturally we had no further jurisdiction." The security man's eyes were cold and accusing, but Walton did not flinch.

"1406?" he repeated. "All right, Martinez. Thanks for your cooperation."

He blanked the screen. He was moving coolly, crisply now. In order to get a mind-pick authorization, he would have to see

President Lanson personally. Very well; he would see President Lanson.

The shrunken old man in the White House was openly deferential to the Popeek head. Walton stated his case quickly, bluntly. Lanson's watery, mild eyes blinked a few times at the many complexities of the situation. He rocked uneasily up and down.

Finally he said, "This mind picking—it's absolutely necessary?"

"Absolutely. We must know where that serum is hidden."

Lanson sighed heavily. "I'll authorize it," he said. He looked beaten.

Washington to New York was a matter of some few minutes. The precious authorization in his hands, Walton spoke to di Cassio via the screener setup at Security Keep, informed him of what was going to be done with him. Then, despite the fat man's hysterical protests, he turned the authorization over to Martinez with instructions to proceed with the mind pick.

It took fifty-eight minutes. Walton waited in a bare, austere office somewhere in the Keep while the mind-picking technicians peeled away the cortex of di Cassio's mind. By now Walton was past all ambivalence, all self-doubt. He thought of himself as a mere robot fulfilling a preset pattern of action.

At 1950 Martinez presented himself before Walton. The little security head looked bleak.

"It's done. Di Cassio's been reduced to blubber and bone. I wouldn't want to watch another mind picking too soon."

"You may have to," Walton said. "If di Cassio wasn't the right one, I intend to go straight down the line on all hundred-odd of them. One of them dealt with Fred. One of them must know where the Lamarre papers are."

Martinez shook his head wearily. "No. There won't need to be any more mind-picking. We got it all out of di Cassio. The transcript ought to be along any moment."

As the security man spoke, an arrival bin in the office flashed and a packet arrived. Walton broke impatiently for the bin, but Martinez waved him away. "This is my domain, Mr. Walton. Please be patient."

With infuriating slowness, Martinez opened the packet, removed some closely-typed sheets, nodded over them. He handed them to Walton.

"Here. Read for yourself. Here's the record of the conversation between your brother and di Cassio. I think it's what you're looking for."

Walton accepted the sheets tensely and began to read:

Di Cassio: *You have a what?*

Fred Walton: *An immortality serum. Eternal life. You know. Some Popeek scientist invented it, and I stole his notebook from my brother's office. It's all here.*

Di Cassio: *Buono! Excellent work. Excellent. Immortality, you say?*

Fred Walton: *Damned right. And it's the weapon we can use to pry Roy out of office. All I have to do is tell him he'd better get out of the way or we'll turn the serum loose on humanity, and he'll move. He's an idealist—stars in his eyes and all that. He won't dare resist.*

Di Cassio: *This is marvelous. You will, of course, send the serum formula to us for safe keeping?*

Fred Walton: *Like hell I will. I'm keeping those notes right where they belong—inside my head. I've destroyed the notebooks and had the scientist killed. The only one who knows the secret is yours truly. This is just to prevent double-crossing on your part, di Cassio. Not that I don't trust you, you understand.*

Di Cassio: *Fred, my boy—*

Fred Walton: *None of that stuff. You gave me a free hand. Don't try to interfere now.*

Walton let the transcript slip from his numb hands to the floor.

"My God," he said softly. "My God!"

Martinez' bright eyes flicked from Walton to the scattered papers on the floor. "What's the trouble? You've got Fred in your custody, haven't you?"

"Didn't you read the order I sent you?"

Martinez chuckled hollowly. "Well, yes—it was a Happysleep authorization. But I thought it was just a way of avoiding that writ ... I mean ... your own *brother*, man?"

"That was no dodge," Walton said. "That was a Happysleep order, and I meant it. Really. Unless there was a slip-up, Fred went to the chamber four hours ago. And," said Walton, "he took the Lamarre formula along with him."

Alone in his office in the night-shadowed Cullen Building, Walton stared at his own distorted reflection mirrored in the opaqued windows. On his desk lay the slip of paper bearing the names of those who had gone to Happysleep in the 1500 gassing.

Frederic Walton was the fourth name on the list. For once, there had been no slip-ups.

Walton thought back over the events of the last nine days. One of his earliest realizations during that time had been that the head of Popeek held powers of life and death over humanity.

Godlike, he had assumed both responsibilities. He had granted life to Philip Prior; that had been the start of this chain of events, and the first of his many mistakes. Now, he had given death to Frederic Walton, an act in itself justifiable, but in consequence the most massive of his errors.

All his scheming had come to naught. Any help now would have to come from without.

Wearily, he snapped on the phone and asked for a connection to Nairobi. The interstellar swap would have to be canceled; Walton was unable to deliver the goods. Fred would have the final smirk yet.

Some minutes later, he got through to McLeod.

"I'm glad you called," McLeod said immediately. "I've been trying to reach you all day. The Dirnan's getting rather impatient; this low gravity is making him sick, and he wants to get going back to his home world."

"Let me talk to him. He'll be able to leave right away."

McLeod nodded and vanished from the screen. The alien visage of Thogran Klayrn appeared.

"I have been waiting for you," the Dirnan said. "You promised to call earlier today. You did not."

"I'm sorry about that," Walton told him. "I was trying to locate the papers to turn over to you."

"Ah, yes. Has it been done?"

"No," Walton said. "The serum doesn't exist any more. The man who invented it is dead, and so is the only other man who knew the formula."

There was a moment of startled silence. Then the Dirnan said, "You assured me delivery of the information."

"I know. But it can't be delivered." Walton was silent a long while, brooding. "The deal's off. There was a mix-up and the man who had the data was—was inadvertently executed today."

"*Today*, you say?"

"Yes. It was an error on my part. A foolish blunder."

"That is irrelevant," the alien interrupted peevishly. "Is the man's body still intact?"

"Why, yes," Walton said, taken off guard. He wondered what plan the alien had. "It's in our morgue right now. But—"

The alien turned away from the screen, and Walton heard him conferring with someone beyond the field of vision. Then the Dirnan returned.

"There are techniques for recovering information from newly dead persons," Thogran Klayrn said. "You have none of these on Earth?"

"Recovering information?" Walton stammered. "No, we don't."

"These techniques exist. Have you such a device as an electroencephalograph on Earth?"

"Of course."

"Then it is still possible to extract the data from this dead man's brain." The alien uttered a wistful wheeze. "See that the body comes to no harm. I will be at your city shortly."

For a moment Walton did not understand.

Then he thought, *Of course. It had to happen this way.*

He realized the rent in the fabric had been bound up, his mistakes undone, his conscience granted a reprieve. He felt absurdly grateful. That all his striving should have been ruined at the last moment would have been intolerable. Now, all was made whole.

"Thanks," he said with sudden fervor. "Thanks!"

---

14 May 2233....

Roy Walton, director of the Bureau of Population Equalization, stood sweltering in the sun at Nairobi Spaceport, watching the smiling people file past him into the towering, golden-hulled ship.

A powerful-looking man holding a small child in his arms came up to him.

"Hello, Walton," he said in a majestic basso.

Walton turned, startled. "Prior!" he exclaimed, after a moment's fumbling.

"And this is my son, Philip," said Prior. "We'll both be going as colonists. My wife's already aboard, but I just wanted to thank you—"

Walton looked at the happy, red-cheeked boy. "There was a medical exam for all volunteer colonists. How did you get the boy through *this* time?"

"Legitimately," Prior said, grinning. "He's a perfectly healthy, normal boy. That potential TB condition was just that—potential. Philip got an A-one health clearance, so it's New Earth and the wide ranges for the Prior family!"

"I'm glad for you," Walton said absently. "I wish I could go."

"Why can't you?"

"Too much work here," Walton said. "If you turn out any poetry up there, I'd like to see it."

Prior shook his head. "I have a feeling I'll be too busy. Poetry's really just a substitute for living, I'm getting to think. I'll be too busy *living* up there to write anything."

"Maybe," said Walton. "I suppose you're right. But you'd better move along. That ship's due to blast pretty soon."

"Right. Thanks again for everything," Prior said, and he and the child moved on.

Walton watched them go. He thought back over the past year. *At least*, he thought, *I made one right guess. The boy deserved to live.*

The loading continued. One thousand colonists would go this first trip, and a thousand more the next day, and a thousand and a thousand more until a billion of Earth's multitudes were on the new world. There was a great deal of paperwork involved in transporting a billion people through space. Walton's desk groaned with a backlog of work.

He glanced up. No stars were visible, of course, in the midday sky, but he knew that New Earth was out there somewhere. And near it, Dirna.

Some day, he thought, *we'll have learned to control our growth. And that will be the day the Dirnans give us back our immortality formula.*

A warning siren sounded suddenly, and ship number one sprang up from Earth, hovered for a few instants on a red pillar of fire, and vanished. Director Walton looked blankly at the place where the ship had been, and, after a moment, turned away. Plenty of work waited for him back in New York.

www.ingramcontent.com/pod-product-compliance
Lightning Source LLC
Chambersburg PA
CBHW030807180526
45163CB00003B/1170